WAKE UP and Smell the !nnovation

stirring up a return on !magination

Written by Philip A. Newbold & Diane Serbin Stover

With Foreword by Larry Keeley Co-Founder, Doblin

Networlding
PUBLISHING

Books and More that Make the World Better

www.Networlding.com

First Networlding Publishing edition 2010

ISBN-13: 978-0983812807

Cover Design by Kelley Taghon
Interior Design by Katie Nordt

Acknowledgments

Memorial Health System is a mid-sized not-for-profit organization located in South Bend, Indiana, originally founded in 1894. This hospital and healthcare company faces the same daily pressures as other mid-sized service-oriented businesses, balancing the needs of many stakeholders while striving to provide the highest quality and maintain low costs.

In 1998, President and CEO Phil Newbold became inspired by the pioneering ideas of Dr. Leland Kaiser, a healthcare futurist. At Dr. Kaiser's urging, Phil sowed the seeds of innovation and R&D as long-term strategies which would strengthen the organization and ultimately become core competencies. His first recruit was Diane Stover, then Vice President of Marketing and now Vice President of Marketing and Innovation Strategy. Since both had a curious side, Phil and Diane were excited about looking outside healthcare to learn new ways of solving problems and seizing opportunities. Their approach developed into one that is easily adoptable by any organization wanting to shape its own future.

So Many To Thank! — From The Authors

Over the years, we pulled in "smart folk" from within Memorial and from outside organizations to build a pathway for innovation that would ultimately position Memorial as more nimble and open to developing innovative solutions for customers. Our most valued external pathfinders along the way have included some of the world's most sophisticated innovation thought leaders: Tom Peters and Valarie Willis of the Tom Peters Company, Tom Stat and the team at IDEO, Stephen Covey and the Franklin Covey organization, Joe Pine and Jim Gilmore of Strategic Horizons, Leland Kaiser and Kaiser & Associates, John Cofano and Ken Graham formerly of Overlake Medical Center, Raj Kothari of Seneca Partners, Dean Carolyn Woo and Professors Matt Bloom and Jim Davis of the University of Notre Dame, and Larry Keeley and the team at Doblin. They make up our innovation discovery "dream team." How lucky are we!?

We've also learned more than we can ever explain from generous professionals at companies we've scouted on "InnoVisits" around the country. Just a few of our really smart friends are: Baxter Corporation, Dupont, MedTronic, Procter and Gamble, Microsoft, WL Gore, Whirlpool, Underwriter's Laboratories, Lands End, WalMart, General Electric, Steelcase, 3M, SAS, and Herman Miller.

We are also grateful for a great group of internal culture developers at Memorial who embraced the concept of "Innovation Everywhere" from the start. Our first thanks go to our longest standing supporters: Mike O'Neil, Chief Operating Officer, Memorial Health System, Matt Krathwohl, Executive Director, George Soper, Ph.D., Chief Learning Officer, and Reg Wagle, Executive Vice President, Memorial Health Foundation. Other invaluable contributors who have come along on the journey over the past 12 years include: Ken Anderson, DO, Kim Smoyer, Lora Tatum, Chris Endres, Tom Merry, Colleen Sweeney, R.N., Julian Lewiecki, Deborah Drendall, Barb Walsh, Diane Dudek-Parmalee, R.N., Johan Kuitse, Rob Riley, M.D., John Albright, R.N., Bev Teegarden, R.N., Jennifer Warfel, and more every day!

We would also like to thank our respective families, who almost always enthusiastically listened to our ideas and our dreams about how we might be able to make a difference in our organization, in our industry, in our world! Their support during the extra time needed as we explored the power of an innovation culture, on the road and beyond the regular work schedule, was one of the greatest gifts and offered great fuel for continued work despite numerous detours along the way.

WITH OUR SINCERE THANKS.
Phil and Diane

Introduction

As a member of a company or organization, you have the inside scoop– your knowledge and skills are unique and valuable to your company. What you may not have considered until now, however, is how valuable your ideas and enthusiasm are as well. Are you a leader? Then we hope to inspire you to look to your team members for their inside information and innovative ideas to make your organization better, more nimble, and more exciting. We, too, are just a couple of everyday leaders with big dreams, loads of curiosity, and a poorly developed sense of what's possible.

Are you a team member? Then this book is for you as well. Learn about the up-and-coming field of "Innovation Strategy": how innovation develops, how it grows, and how it can help your organization flourish in a competitive environment.

This book chronicles the discovery and innovation as a success strategy by an independent service organization. We happen to be in the healthcare field; however the lessons we have to share apply to any industry. How we wake up to the strengthening of power of a culture of innovation and the impact that is followed is a story that can help others in many types of business. Wake Up & Smell the Innovation became our way of framing how startling, how unexpected and how immersive the journey can be when building an innovation culture. We're passionate about the multidimensional benefits and look forward to our real-life story helping and Wake-Up as well.

We stepped back and looked at the world around us. We looked within our field for ideas about how to stop simply reacting to outside influences; instead, we wanted to proactively create our desired future. When we weren't inspired by the practices we found, we knew that our step back needed to become a step forward instead. Opening our minds to creative strategies from outside our field led us on an exciting journey. We hope our journey inspires you to explore and apply new ideas and innovations in your business.

In this book, we will share everything we did and experienced, good and bad, but your adventure will be unique and completely your own. Our adventure was launching an "Innovation Revolution." We hope you also launch an Innovation Revolution, reenergize your career, put life and meaning back into work, and, as Tom Peters says "make work cool again."

We've organized our book similarly to a manual, beginning with an outline that explains how an "Innovation Project" works from start to finish. We give you an overview not simply of our process, but of the "Innovation atmosphere." Whereas many seminars on Innovation Strategy are like guides for an engine – important, intricate, but not enough to make the airplane actually move – this book is more of a pilot's manual. Not only will you learn all about the important bits and pieces of the vehicle, but you get to fly into the Innovation Atmosphere at your own pace, altitude, and speed.

Therefore, consider the first few chapters a countdown to takeoff. We begin with some orientation, then jumpstart with two crucial points, and then give you three danger warnings about possible "plagues" that could infect your company. Then we get into the four corners of the plan – where to begin. Next, we'll give you the scoop we wish we had when we began this journey – the five key lessons we learned over the last 12 years making Innovation one of our core competencies. There are plenty of moments showing "Innovation in Action," times when we've used the very methods we're explaining, and highlights from our meetings and projects with other innovative companies, what we call "InnoVisits." We pull out the most essential lesson we learned from each of these and compile them into a list of "prescriptions" you can find at the end of the book.

By Chapter Five, you're ready to take off and let your organization feel the lift of the Innovation atmosphere. This is where you pick up SPEED on the runway: Strategy & Structure, Processes, Environment, Execution, and Dollars/ROI. These chapters outline how to ensure you have the support of your organization and an effective project development and evaluation system.

Innovation should not be daunting or mystifying. We use everyday items you might find in your home; as symbols to identify various segments on how to develop an innovation strategy. They are inexpensive, everyone has used them, and they help us demystify Innovation and make it simple, understandable, memorable, accessible, and fun. We integrate many of the business practices and models you already know (such as Quality Improvement, Covey's Seven Lessons, Six Sigma and Lean), but we look at them through the lens of Innovation.

Our basic definition of an Innovative culture is an environment where abundant problem-solving ideas are welcomed, tested, refined, and then put into action. With that in mind, take a moment to consider the potential of a more Innovative culture in your organization. Think about what might make customers and your team members feel more secure, less afraid, even possibly cherished.

Chapter Guide

1 – 3 = How do you think about and understand the power of Innovation?

4 & 5 = Preparatory steps to take before moving into the action phase.

6 – 10 = Your direct path to Monday morning implementation.

Foreword

By Larry Keeley

When teams first agree that they need innovation there is a palpable sense of excitement. The assumption is that *innovation will be fun*, especially compared to that boring regular stuff we have to do every day. *Surely this will be our chance to be creative, go nuts and invent stuff. Hey, we'll be like Apple!*

Smart, highly motivated people are stuck in a room. Toys are festooned all around the tables. Someone in the front reminds the participants that *There is no such thing as a bad idea!*

Then the indignities begin.

Enthusiastic participants generate hundreds of ideas. Some will secretly inject old Rodney Dangerfield-class ideas that have been long discredited and don't get no respect. People make impassioned speeches: *Yeah, this time, we are gonna get it right…* The excitement is palpable. We all get to vote with sticky dots.

Sometimes after this highly caffeinated beginning all such teams hit a wall. In some cases it takes less than a day. Others will take weeks, even months. But eventually reality rises and asserts itself. This is when you discover that real innovation is a tough nut. In the overwhelming number of cases, when it gets tough, teams abandon the tasks. In all too many of those, they quietly conclude that *We tried that innovation thing and we're just not good at it around here*. Then the enterprise has a toxic allergic reaction to the topic, one that will persist for several years, until a new team comes in and the cycle begins anew.

More than you can possibly imagine, this surly little pattern is the norm when enterprises try to innovate. But it's not what happened at Memorial Hospital & Health System. Under the leadership of Phil Newbold, this team started innovating with the usual enthusiasm and hit more than one wall. The difference is they persisted. They went on lots of trips to other firms to catalogue their practices and find their patterns. They built an unprecedented collection of the best advisors – and somehow managed to politely suffer through the conflicting advice of all those "experts." They consistently worked to indentify breakdowns and flip them into breakthroughs.

So here's the deal. Maybe *you* are getting ready to innovate. Or perhaps you are already down the road a way and have discovered the painful truth that there really are bad ideas. Perhaps you catch occasional glimpses when the journey shifts from initial excitement to something more than the Bataan Death March. Your colleagues aren't happy. The outcomes aren't pretty. People quietly scrub any mention of their innovation projects off their CVs. These are the symptoms that you need a different way forward.

If you persist, you're faced with the critical challenge of building your own fusion of innovation practices that will work in your firm and with your team. You need to make innovation your own.

Here's what Phil and Diane know: If you treat creative ideas like the answer without disciplined execution you seem childish. If you are courageous without realism you seem reckless. If you are ambitious without patience you seem delusional. Great innovation is plagued with these perils and it demands great persistence.

In this slim book they tell the tale of how they made innovation their own. How they flipped adversity to advantage, and what they did to make Memorial Hospital & Health System a powerhouse of innovation that punches way above its weight.

Read it. Savor it. Steal from it. With a little luck and a lot of effort it can help your team bravely scale all those walls they will inevitably hit when they work to innovate.

Larry Keeley
Co-Founder, Doblin Inc.
Group Leader, Monitor Innovation

CHAPTER 1
Orientation and the Wake-Up Call

In order to get ready for the exciting adventure ahead, let's prepare ourselves with some key terms and qualities you and your company need to develop or possess in order to tackle an Innovation Revolution.

One should not jump into an airplane without first learning the gears and safety measures. Plus, you need to be speaking the same language as others in the cockpit and cabin to operate within it. This chapter draws together the essential ideas that many authors, researchers, and consultants have developed into a useful framework for understanding Innovation and for effectively engaging leaders to use Innovation as a key change strategy for the future. Much as a compass is essential for orienting to a certain direction, the following are definitions and ways of thinking about Innovation that can help leaders prepare their organizations for new directions.

Creating Definitions
Every person and every organization should go through the process of arriving at an individualized definition of Innovation before moving forward and developing the broader team. Not only does this allow you to create a clear goal for your revolution, but the exercise of thinking through the various facets and variations of Innovation is also helpful as an interactive demonstration of how complex and

often misperceived the practice really is. Consider beginning in the same way as many other writers on ideation and Innovation have — with a three-part explanation of the term.

- First, there is always something about what's "new" — new ideas, new models, new thinking, new products, new benefits, new services, etc. However, "new" has its own challenges as well: New to whom? How new? Same as invention?
- Second, the definition always includes action, adoption, and implementation rather than simply an idea or model. This separates Innovation from its close companion, "ideation." Ideation has its place when generating models, but the notion here is that the "new" actively gets implemented and used. So, the verb form "to innovate" is just as important as the noun "innovation."
- Third, Innovation must drive value to a customer who uses or needs it. It can lead to a competitive advantage, contributing to success for an individual or organization.

After considering these various requirements, we arrived at the following definition.

Innovation (noun or verb)
A new idea or model that, when implemented, proves valuable to a customer or leads to a competitive advantage.

Pretty simple and straightforward, right? An important aspect here is that the definition bubbled up from the people who created it. This needs to be true for the definition your team develops as well; it needs to fit your organization and industry. Engagement, interactivity, and ownership are always a great way to start any new initiative and adventure.

Dev Patniak, CEO of Jump in California, has been one of our trusted advisors. He shared another useful definition of what's important to be an innovator. In the illustration below, Dev features three components of an Innovation culture. A unique point from this model is that his team emphasizes the need to be empathetic before the creative process begins. As with many other models, execution or putting ideas into action is also a crucial part of the process. Innovation is not about simple creativity. It's mostly about energetically testing, trying, and implementing.

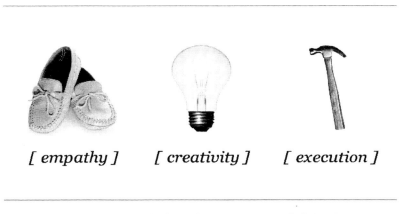

[empathy]   [creativity]   [execution]

USED WITH PERMISSION FROM DEV PATNAIAK, CEO JUMP

Now, let's look at some of the components and major players in the field of Innovation Strategies as it currently stands.

The Three C's: Competency, Culture, and Courage

One of the wisest and most important mentors we met on our adventure was Larry Keeley of Monitor-Doblin based in Chicago. Doblin has been the premier Innovation Strategy firm with dozens of Fortune 100 engagements and a cutting-edge Innovation ideology that often flies in the face of established practice. Keeley is a frequent speaker at many of the top Innovation conferences, and regularly receives standing ovations for his keen insights, vast research-based knowledge, and good humor. Often, he condenses complex and contradictory discussions of Innovation topics into three major points. We have used these three "C's" dozens of times to orient ourselves during chaotic times and to quickly teach others just beginning their journey.

Essentially, Innovation must be a **competency** that becomes an integral part of your organization's **culture**. The process of making it so requires **courage**.

COMPETENCY

First and foremost, Innovation is a competency that must be learned much like the theories, bodies of knowledge, principles, methodologies, and tools of quality improvement and customer service. What do we mean by competency?

> **Competency (noun)**
> *The combination of knowledge, skills, personal characteristics, and individual and social behaviors needed to perform a job.*
> **Antonyms:** *inability, limitation, paralysis*

Nobody is born with an "Innovation gene," but the good news is that everybody can get better at being more innovative, more creative, and more imaginative. While some people appear to be more innovative than others (often called more "right brained"), Innovation needs to be studied, practiced and learned by the leadership in every organization if they are going to be competitive, thriving, and successful in the future.

CULTURE

We believe all growth in organizations comes from project work. Typical project teams work in a linear fashion and focus on tangible steps along the way. Early on we decided to adopt the WOW Project Methodology developed by Tom Peters. Wow Projects involve a focus on tangibles and intangibles such as passion and emotion to help teams truly move beyond mediocrity. Before you begin requiring Innovation training or starting WOW projects, take the time to assess your current status – who you are as an organization and how that will affect your progress in Innovation. Essentially, be aware of and continuously monitor your culture (see more on how to do this in Chapter 8).

> **Culture (noun)**
> *Loosely equivalent to "the way we do things around here," it is vital to any organization's success and has a tremendous impact on its most important asset: talent and human capital.*

Nearly every organization wants a culture that is positive, supportive, teachable, and empowering. Plus, Innovation works best in a culture that possesses these characteristics. An Innovative culture supports new thinking and risk-taking, enables leaders to see new possibilities, is crucial for the problem-solving process, and allows experimentation, rapid discovery, and deep learning.

COURAGE

You can't prove in advance precisely what will result from Innovation. This means that Innovation requires leaders to display great courage because they are often challenging the status quo, including long-standing practices and methods.

> **Courage (noun)**
> *1. The ability to face uncertainty, failure, and success with enthusiasm*
> *2. Bravery; valor.*
> **Antonyms:** *fear, timidity, weakness, meekness*

Leaders are often opening themselves to possible failures when promoting crazy new ideas that don't always work. To some, this is what causes the Innovation process to appear too risky and uncertain. What may surprise such critics, however, is that leaders often incur the greatest risks when they allow their organizations to stagnate, becoming uncompetitive, uninteresting places to work, and ultimately unsuccessful. In today's volatile economic environment, leaders need real courage to begin the process of transforming their organizations, their communities and their economies. Since transformations and innovations take some time to accomplish, begin now; it's always the right time to take full advantage of the future.[i]

Innovation in Action: Microsoft's Dr. Goodwell

In the early days, we had more questions about Innovation than answers. Curiosity, an important trait for innovative people or companies, drove a great deal of our research. For example Diane, our Vice President of Marketing received a magazine with a small article about how Microsoft was beginning to explore a system allowing doctors to do simple visits online with patients. At the time, it was a wild idea; however, we persisted in seeing how we might adapt that idea, mustering the courage to reach out and learn. We were receptive to and energized by wild ideas, an important characteristic that helped us on our journey.

We wove our way through the maze of Microsoft to find the project champion for what was then called "Dr. Goodwell." John Cofano at Overlake Medical Center in Bellevue, Washington was full of energy and excitement about the possibilities of this new approach to primary care medicine. He introduced us to his medical advisors and, during our first conference call with the chief innovators at Overlake, we discovered there were at least two other souls searching for the magic that Innovation might offer hospitals. Bill Crounse, M.D., and Ken Graham, the CEO, were on a similar path to ours. We hosted the Microsoft Dr. Goodwell team at Memorial hoping we might help launch this service to the world.

Unfortunately, the medical environment just wasn't ready yet. Still, despite this disappointment, we ended up with insights and experience about a new product, we learned a great deal by observing another group's Innovation journey, and we added three great members to our "smart friend" list.

Years later we learned that although the original plan to have Dr. Goodwell in office settings (so staff members wouldn't have to leave work for minor doctor visits) was unsuccessful, it reemerged for another use: as a timeshare business for Americans who became ill during travel. The original concept was simply before its time, but we look forward to round two someday soon.

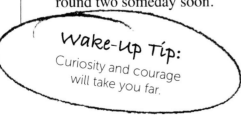

Wake-Up Tip:
Curiosity and courage will take you far.

Is All Innovation the Same? Divide and Conquer

Larry Keeley and Doblin also helped form our understanding of Innovation Strategy by breaking it into categories and types.[ii] Most Innovations can be thought of as falling into one of the following major categories, depending on how they impact your organization. Each category of Innovations has a role to play in your overall strategy.

SUSTAINING INNOVATIONS

These innovations should make up approximately seventy percent of your projects; they can preserve existing offerings or extend the lifespan of products and services. This happens since most organizations easily embrace the ability to prompt incremental innovations but it's more complex and involved to achieve radical innovations. You might look at the difference as similar to the likeliness of hitting singles regularly and home runs once in awhile. Sustaining innovations include quality and product improvements and implementation of LEAN or Six Sigma. Often, this means pursuing efficiencies that lower costs or improve quality but can be duplicated. A sustaining Innovation introduced by one organization quickly becomes an industry standard, and the firm loses its ability to differentiate itself from the competition. Online package tracking is an example in the logistics industry. Another example is the introduction of frequent flier programs for airlines.

TRANSFORMATIONAL INNOVATIONS

These projects, SHOULD make up about twenty percent of your Innovation pipeline since these can take longer and involve more significant change and may include several operational elements such as combining products and services to provide more important differentiation from competitors. Lasik surgery, done on an outpatient basis, is a transformational Innovation that affected patients, optometrists, and eyeglass makers in addition to surgical ophthalmologists. Hybrid cars, along with the recent increase in gasoline prices, may well have a transformational effect on automobile design and construction.

REVOLUTIONARY INNOVATIONS

While usually only ten percent of your projects are revolutionary Innovations, they do occur at a still-higher level, affecting companies and entire industries. These

Innovations have such a profound impact on economics and customer preferences that they remake the competitive landscape. A prime example in healthcare is the emergence of freestanding ambulatory diagnostic and surgical centers. Given the opportunity to receive services in these venues, patients not requiring hospitalization quickly migrated to more customer-friendly "focused factories." Similarly, ethanol has revolutionized the way cars are made and marketed, as well as reviving agricultural production.

The Innovation Atmosphere

During one of our early site visits to benchmark Innovation (InnoVisits), we went to Baxter International. CEO Harry Kraemer made an important distinction about different types of Innovations. Since that time, we have used this categorization hundreds of times with both external and internal groups, to great effect. Baxter separates Innovation into three types:

NEW TO THE ORGANIZATION

This is the world of existing best practices currently in place in other organizations, but which appear brand new to your organization. There are many institutions, conferences, consultants, and management books all identifying and providing examples of alleged best practices. These are meant to help organizations improve their performance without individually having to go out and conduct research. The most well known group in the healthcare area is the Advisory Board Company, which uses a lengthy series of phone interviews, panels of experts, and market research to present trends and best practices to the field.

Most leaders are quite familiar with this type of Innovation; it is the bedrock of most industry conferences, seminars, webinars, and trade shows. All organizations need to regularly identify best practices in every product, service, and department in order to understand why and how they can be better.

Generally, most of these best practices are incremental or management-related, and few represent radical or breakthrough Innovations. Although the pathways for adopting best practices vary field by field (see Chapter 8), in many areas a poor system of diffusion can lead to pockets of improvement but no widespread change. To keep an organization vibrant, everyone needs to be apprised of continuing progress and improving standards within the field.

Innovation in Action: The "Red Zone"

One of our nursing directors attended an educational event outside the hospital and returned with a brilliant idea: the Red Zone. The purpose of the Zone is to provide nurses with an interruption-free space to prepare their patients' medications in an effort to improve concentration and accuracy.

The nursing director adapted insights from the event she attended and developed a prototype on her unit. She quickly turned a storage area into a locked room that contains only the necessary supplies and equipment for medication preparation. The space included a computer, medication refrigerator, automated medication dispensing machine, and pharmacy drop-off box.

The director also developed "Red Zone Rules" to regulate the space: these are a set of behaviors that, if practiced, increase the ability of staff to "be in the moment" while preparing medications in the Red Zone. These behaviors included not talking to or otherwise bothering nurses (unless for an emergency) while they are preparing medications. A painted a red stripe around the room reinforced the purpose.

Since implementing the concept, other nursing directors have modeled the Red Zone on their floors and it is now a key component of maintaining patient safety at Memorial.

When we began our Innovation journey, we were unprepared for the impact of letting loose 3600 employees into the Innovation atmosphere.

Over time we have learned how to provide support and resources for suggested projects. Despite initial challenges, the results were undeniably worth the initial risk.

Wake-Up Tip:
Innovation is a team effort.

NEW TO THE INDUSTRY

Memorial occupies a particular niche: we go out to identify Innovations that are currently in place in other industries. In fact, this has been the major focus of our efforts over the past five years. Most of our efforts have been to learn what other innovative companies have accomplished through their decades of trial and error, large research and development (R&D) expenditures and experience with global competition. We have then taken these early lessons from our InnoVisits and adapted them to our healthcare setting applying them everywhere possible.

Most of the organizations we visited have stayed somewhat involved with us because they want to share lessons and build a growing potential "test bed" and partnership network. These organizations are genuinely interested in — even passionate about — Innovation. Often, innovative companies can offer advice concerning their journeys, share their experiences and insights, and offer to be speakers at management conferences and board retreats.

Therefore, consider learning more about their ideation process — their process for taking an idea all the way through to a working prototype. Learn about the teams and champions who work on new ideas, about incentives and recognition systems, and about associated cultural transformations. Since these companies have been successful for decades, analyzing their discovery process helps speed the learning curve of your leadership. It is affirming for those just beginning the Innovation journey, and offers tangible evidence that the tools, processes and culture really work. In sum, it is vital for long-term success.

NEW TO THE WORLD

This is the world of invention, the output of large R&D labs, or the brainchild of the persistent entrepreneur. Bringing a new product, service, or idea into the world and making it a success is indeed a difficult and messy undertaking. Memorial has taken the position that this is not our niche or expertise, but rather we would like to partner with those extraordinary companies who have a rich, regular flow of new models, new products, and new services each year. It is doubtful that a nurse working on the 8th floor, a lab or radiology tech in one of our physician practices, or an ER physician is going to invent the next Post-it™ note, duct tape, or Velcro™. However, in order to be a player in this world of invention, we have developed partnerships with several organizations needing ready access to our clinical staff as a test bed for new prototypes and models. We help speed the timelines to an invention's market success. These partnerships often are developed in the Memorial Venture Center (See Chapter 6), and many require a written contractual agreement setting out the roles of each partner, the revenue sharing, and the ownership of intellectual property and assets.

Innovation in Action: Nike – A Fabulous Failure

To see failure as the missed opportunity for trying something new is to also see failure from an Innovation perspective. This is the case with Memorial's exploration of a new service Innovation from Nike. After an InnoVisit at the company, our organizations were eager for additional dialogue in order to explore a possible strategic alliance. In particular, we discussed what is now known as the Nike Sensory Sports Training (Nike SST), currently being offered at the Michael Johnson Performance Center in McKinney, Texas.

Nike SST is state-of-the-art vision training for today's athletes. Nike SST sport vision training lab puts elite athletes through a battery of visual tests to set a baseline for their vision, peripheral vision, depth perception, and timing abilities. Different visual exercises are then incorporated into the training regimen to strengthen vision, reaction and accuracy. The Nike SST lab can be key for many athletes achieving the next performance level.

The Project Champion from Memorial was confident that Memorial would serve as a great laboratory to further test SST, using Memorial's expertise and relationships in sports medicine and leveraging our retail experience. However despite several attempts to finalize collaboration plans, Nike eventually moved on and so did Memorial.

While we never GOT THE project with Nike OFF THE GROUND, the lessons were STILL invaluable and include:

- Learning about how important Innovation is to achieving the mission.
- Learning about how Nike pursues innovation.
- What Innovation methodologies and tools the company used.
- Learning about the Nike "Maxims" or Nike's brand mission which is to bring inspiration and innovation to every athlete in the world.
- Learning about Nike's process for new business venture formations such as Nike Towns and Micro Loans.
- Learning about Nike's Innovation Kitchen where they work on future offerings.
- Learning when to move a project to the cryotank or holding area if the environment isn't yet ready for its launch.

Wake-Up Tip: Cultivate diverse partnerships.

Partnerships with inventive companies provide an organization with exposure to a wide range of new ideas. As well as the opportunity to think about Innovation in a new way, organizations also gain a chance to seek partners, build networks, and accumulate a broad base of support. Since Innovation is largely a contact sport, there is no reason to go it alone. Much of the magic of Silicon Valley, the Research Triangle in Raleigh-Durham, and the Boston 128 corridor is the contact, sharing, and inter-action across companies. The product is a macro incubator that allows a culture of Innovation to thrive. Any organization beginning to learn about Innovation should build a large sharing network to enrich its learning and ultimate results.

The Wake-Up Call

When we're soundly asleep, sometimes we need a wake-up call to rouse us and help us reconnect with the world. Being jarred awake also reorients us, inspiring us to action. Often, without a wake-up call, we would have continued sleeping, missing opportunities. Ask yourself, "Is your company asleep?" Twelve years ago, we would have answered in the affirmative, but not anymore. Twelve years ago, we heard our wake-up call: a simple, apparently innocuous question that nevertheless worked like an alarm. It was simply, "Why don't Hospital and Health Systems have R&D policies and Innovation functions?"

The question was posed by a rather unlikely Innovation hero whose ideas were buzzing through the halls and offices of hospitals all across America via his inspi-rational seminars and speeches. Dr. Kaiser, a healthcare futurist, mentor, coach, speaker, author, and a great friend of Memorial has been incessantly travelling the entire country, five days a week, 40+ weeks a year for decades trying to encourage hospital leadership to expand their consciousness, consider alternative futures, and to bring spirituality into both healing processes and leaders' everyday lives. His early focus was on how to aspire to build healthier communities. In the early 90s Leland began talking about the need for an R&D policy within every hospital in America. He advocated setting aside resources to invest in reinventing, redesign-ing, and reimagining a more enlightened future that creates health for the entire community. Dr. Kaiser passionately started to push us to be more proactive and less reactive about the future. He also pushed us to apply the creative sides as much as our analytical sides of our brains to build a vital and relevant organization.

Kaiser's apparently simple question inspired us to get a jumpstart on our future: we began investigating R&D policies, the process of Innovation, and the ways in which new ideas could benefit a hospital and its patients. We weren't the only ones reacting; the alarm on the clock was getting louder and louder as American industry began to embrace Innovation as a core competency for any successful enterprise. Literature seemed full of articles praising the merits of Innovation and the promise of new ideas and whole new business models. Creative thinking and ideation became buzzwords almost overnight as dozens of books and business articles implored leaders to "think out of the box," to "brainstorm," and to "blue sky-it."

We were a willing audience for this whirlwind of information and creativity, but we ensured that we weren't swept in a direction inappropriate for our organization. We were always willing to listen, but with a careful ear to how practices best suited our needs, rather than trying each trend as it came.

Organizational wake-ups normally arise after one of two situations. The first is a major setback such as losing your largest customer to another organization with higher quality, better customer services, or new products with improved features and benefits. Second, a wake-up could result from a major financial crisis which, in hindsight, was some years in the making. Occasionally, some organizations stay out ahead of the latest crisis and spot key trends and big customer shifts before they overtake tried and proven business models. Whether through keen insight, intuitive leadership, or just plain luck, a few businesses are inspired to change before they are forced to do so by an unforgiving marketplace. As Tony Robbins, a lecturer in Innovation, often says, "People change out of either inspiration or desperation!"

As a leader of an Innovation Revolution, you have to decide on which side of the coin you want to place your organization's bets. Personally, we advise you take this moment to be inspired. After all, inspiration gives you a head start in selecting when and how to launch new products or services, thereby allowing you the use of more resources under less pressure.

Another responsibility of an Innovation leader is to be understanding of those less enthusiastic about the endeavor. After all, one of the reasons why Innovation seems so foreign and difficult for many leaders is the absence of any skill building and practice in this emerging new competency. Many of those holding a leadership position or title got where they are today by excelling in linear thinking, problem solving, inductive and deductive reasoning, and skilled analysis (all left-brained functions). After 15+ years in school and 20+ years on the job, leftbrained thinking and analysis have almost systemically excluded any competency in rightbrained activities (imagination, intuition, creativity, curiosity, and conceptual thinking).[iii]

In kindergarten when the five and six-year-olds are asked, "Who in the class are artists, poets, and musicians?" all the hands in the class go up with great enthusiasm. Take that same class thirteen years later when they are posing for the senior class picture. When asked, "Who in the class are artists, poets or musicians?" you might have three brave souls raising their hands. In thirteen years we seem to have beaten the creativity and right-brained thinking out of our children in favor of almost exclusively left-brained problem solving, analysis, logic, and deductive reasoning. Fast forward another 15+ years in a typical quantitative-thinking organization and we find even more entrenched left-brained leaders with almost no development of the right-brain functions of creativity, imagination and intuition. It's almost as though we have raised an entire generation of leaders who have been furiously "pumping iron" with their left arm until it resembles an Olympic weightlifter's, but through neglect and disuse, their right arm looks like that of a stereotypical computer scientist. We don't want any less rigorous left-brained analysis, problem solving, and linear thinking in the future, but we need far more attention to building up and developing our creative, intuitive, imaginative right brain if we are to be more effective and balanced leaders for the rapidly changing future.

Our first step in building our innovative skills was to search within the healthcare provider industry. After many calls and searches, we learned there were no clear models to follow. This was a critical point that started us looking outside of our own industry.

We began an intensive review of the literature and started our first InnoVisits (see Chapter 4) as a way to find out more about these seemingly mysterious R&D labs, full of intellectual property, the promise of patents and licensing streams of revenue, and brilliant scientists and thinkers. Beyond hospitals and health system delivery organizations, we were struck by how Innovation was permeating all sectors of business and industry. There were only three glaring exceptions, and they were all in the tax-exempt, non-profit sector: government, education, and religion.

First, we found no evidence of R&D functions in government at any level (local, state or federal). There were no line items in government budgets to re-imagine or reinvent forms of representation, governance duties, or ways of delivering essential public service. In fact, many forms of local township government still exist almost untouched after more than 150 years, in spite of the advancements of the internet, regionalization, and shifting demographics.

Secondly, education at the local and state levels has remarkably escaped the Innovation Revolution sweeping most sectors of American industry. Whether due to a thicket of regulation, influence of organized labor, poor school funding formulas, or changing family structures, it is hard to identify any resources set aside each year that go toward redesigning the student educational experience or the teaching/learning methods. Some charter and private schools have interesting experiments underway to help demonstrate improved student outcomes, but no systematic and pervasive R&D functions exist anywhere.

Thirdly, organized religion is remarkably devoid of innovative thinking, with one growing exception: mega churches. It is not uncommon to find resources invested by these mega churches in recreating a more interactive, engaging religious experience for the thousands who flock to the dozen separate religious services offered on a typical Sunday. These charismatic pastors and their church leadership borrow freely from many different industries – entertainment, music, the arts, and communications – tore-imagine a whole new religious experience built upon the same doctrines, teachings, and rituals as many other traditional churches.

Since organizations so integral to our way of life resist Innovation, skepticism is to be expected from your team members. In fact, as you begin to talk about launching an Innovation Revolution, you will hear frequent and concerned questions from your colleagues and staff: "Why are we starting this Innovation thing anyway?," "We are doing pretty well without it, aren't we?," "We are already overwhelmed with quality and customer service initiatives, can't we just get these mastered before we take on anything else?," and "Is anybody going to pay us more for these Innovations, and what's the return on investment for Innovation anyway?"

These are smart questions from skeptical workers who may already be stressed and overwhelmed from downsizing, outsourcing, or global competition. Leaders of the revolution had better have sharp, compelling, and credible answers, or they risk a growing cynicism over another "flavor of the month" initiative. You can temper your argument for change by stressing the fact that established models (which may have been created by the very people you're trying to convince) simply need to be moved forward. By emphasizing growth rather than abandonment, you may encourage more willing participation from hesitant team members. Still, the move-ment can and should go on with or without their support. If naysayers remain, try to get them involved in a project if possible. Even if they decline and stand back for a period, always assure them that they can join the Innovation movement at any time.

So where do you go when facing such resistance? As we said earlier, courage is necessary, as is knowledge of your culture. Therefore, the starting point for any organization willing to transform itself into a more innovative, creative, and nimble enterprise begins with a sobering assessment of its current situations. Only when an organization's leaders are dissatisfied with the status quo (i.e., their current com-petitiveness and probable future in a quickly changing market), do organizations have any hope of large-scale change and transformation.

Organizational assessments paint a realistic picture of the current competitive land-scape and accomplish three important goals.

1. **Doing the Math:** Unless there is enough dissatisfaction, worry, and angst about the current situation (success measures, competitiveness, viability, an uncertain future), leaders cannot overcome the inertia and habits of their organization and its culture to chart a new future and a new direction. Until the pressure to change inside a person or an organization is greater than the cost of uncertainty and risk of a whole new way of thinking and operating, change simply does not happen.

2. **Testing the Waters:** An objective assessment with a wide variety of tools, measures and benchmarks provides not only a jumping-off point to a new direction but also serves to measure progress and accomplishment for the new way. Whether these important metrics are for individuals in leadership or cover the organization's status (see Chapter 4), it is incredibly important to have solid data, great diagnostics, and real sense of where you are situated before you can begin change.

3. **Diffusing and Enthusing:** Third, as with any change initiative, your employees and staff will want to know why the current pathway and direction needs to change. A wellcrafted message based on credible data and an honest assessment of the status quo and the likely future is essential if change is going to occur rapidly and throughout the entire enterprise.

You've already had the wake-up call. (You are reading this book, after all.) Now, let's test the waters and get to know your culture. There are several assessments that help an organization as it begins the Innovation adventure. Many of these have the additional benefit of spreading awareness and pride regarding the new competency.

Innovation Presence – Releasing Individual Innovation Potential

Everyone is capable of being innovative, coming up with new and imaginative ways of doing things, but too often we hear people remark that they are not. So how do we assist people to see that they have the innate ability to innovate? First, there may be barriers to people's perception of who can innovate; they worry that they don't possess the necessary academic credentials or that they don't "know enough." On the other hand, if they do have the credentials, they may think they already know enough and believe there is nothing of relevance outside that knowledge.

Other barriers include disciplinary boundaries that can restrict people's movement, as well as perceived lack of opportunity to innovate within a particular job class. All of these barriers are artificial and hide real innovative talent awaiting release. So how do we assist people to see and believe that they have the capacity to be innovative? And then how do we help them tap into that capacity? We'll discuss this in Chapter Four when we talk about assembling your team.

Increasing the Capacity for Innovation

Many of the characteristics of Innovation are as much learned as innate and, as we said before, Innovation can be developed. At Memorial, individuals who exhibit strong innovative tendencies and have strong "Innovation Presence" are invited to attend more intensive WOW training and assigned to specific projects. Others with less strong "Innovation Presence" are assigned a mentor who is actively engaged in Innovation projects. In addition, the characteristics of Innovation that may be lacking in a manager are identified and means of improvement are sought.

CEOs play a key part in identifying and inspiring the Innovation team. As well as understanding weaknesses with the status quo, the CEO has additional responsibilities as the most visible leader. He or she must be strongly supportive of the initial exploration and its leader. Without such high-level commitment, shorter-term thinkers will quickly abandon the messy path of building Innovation competencies. Having a CEO who embraces a long-term perspective and who is willing to support efforts to keep an organization relevant in the future is critical. Preferably, the CEO should lead the effort to enhance the Innovation profile, but a CEO who will designate and protect exploration by less senior enthusiasts is also a great start.

Building a Sense of Urgency

After devising a system to identify and organize innovators, take advantage of them to build a sense of urgency in the corporation. The CEO and senior leadership could start the movement, inspire the Innovation team, and then allow the movement to diffuse into the broader organization. After all, without a keen sense of urgency, most organizational leadership is skeptical of new initiatives and enthusiasm, eventually falling back to the status quo.

Innovation helps most organizations turn up their internal "clock speed" so that problems and opportunities are quickly addressed without the endless meetings and arguments, without the layers of bureaucracy and their slow approvals, and without all the friction, hassles, and naysaying. One good way to help instigate a new sense of urgency is to begin using "Blackjack" meetings wherever possible.

Time is Valuable

Blackjack meetings are simply meetings that last 21 minutes, period. There are at least three reasons why they work so well. First, the 21-minute limit forces attendees to hone their messages and get to the crux of what's important. Second, they signal a new sense of urgency and a new way of doing things that have come out of the new Innovation initiatives (it's applying the Innovation process to reinvent something as basic as a meeting). Third, it will help demonstrate how management can free up valuable time so that leadership has more time to devote to the Innovation teams and their projects.

Wake-Up Tip:
C-suite support is crucial!

Our wake-up call certainly worked; once we began our adventure, a sense of momentum developed as we recognized the importance of bringing in new ideas, new perspectives, and new models of thinking in order to keep our important strategies and initiatives fresh, exciting, and cutting-edge. Innovation became a way of life as we learned about the importance of turning up the organization's clock speed and the value of being nimble, curious, fearless, and focused. Once awake and with no snooze button in sight, it was exciting to be in the midst of our self-imposed race to create a revolution.

CHAPTER 2
Two Anchors in the Future

As you begin your Innovation adventures, it is helpful to have a couple of anchor points to provide stability and support. What we suggest is to establish early on two anchors planted firmly in the future, which should help prevent backsliding and a natural longing to return to the comfortable and familiar past. Senior leaders should use these two anchors to constantly orient their teams and staff towards the critical points.

Since the beginning of the national Innovation Revolution we've been discussing, the literature has emphasized using the unusual to create the extraordinary. "Get out of the box," is often used to encourage this type of thinking. Using quirky team building exercises and thought games also allows you to push your mind out of a rut and think of new solutions. While we have utilized many of these techniques, our methods follow a careful process. We also have established systems to manage the innovation effort. Our managers learn how to play, but with a focus.

Our focus revolves around the teachings of two specific leaders. Their words correlated with our early work on Innovation, and we have found them to be useful guides ever since. Now that you've identified your culture, we offer these lessons to you as well. Share them with your team, post them on a wall in your Innovation space, or just tab this page of the book. When you reach a roadblock, you can return to these quotes for help navigating.

Anchor 1: Albert Einstein's Perspective on Innovation

When Einstein was a boy, his father gave him a compass as a gift. He was fascinated and focused his intellectual energy on solving its riddles. How did it work? What could make the needle move? What larger forces affected its operation? In today's Innovation language, we would say he was "thinking big."

As he grew older, Einstein continued to think big. While some scholars have said that he was a poor student, others contend that he was merely focused. He worked hardest at those subjects he enjoyed: math, physics and playing the violin.[iv] He ignored other subjects (some teachers even thought him unintelligent). However, he began to challenge them in what became his areas of expertise; in fact, he would ask his math instructors questions they were unable to answer. As a teacher struggled to solve the problem he had posed, erasing and re-erasing the chalkboard, the boy sat in the back of the classroom, his smile widening as he recognized the brink of the unknown.

In his book, $E=mc^2$, author David Bodanis outlines the key to Einstein's "big idea" about relativity; Bodanis posits that it was Einstein's ability to view a problem in a whole new way that enabled him to succeed where others had failed. To the detriment of his other courses and later his marriage, Einstein was narrowly focused on explaining natural forces. However, within this field of physics, his view was vast.

Einstein combined previously disparate discoveries into a cohesive whole, bringing together ideas from Antoine Lavoisier, Michael Faraday, and James Clark Maxwell. (They worked on mass, electromagnetism, and light, respectively.) He then applied advanced mathematics. Einstein's predecessors provided him with the raw materials he needed to work. However, his brilliance enabled him to take these materials and reorient them. He established that matter is simply a form of energy, and can be converted into other forms such as light. Matter and energy are related through a specific formula, $E=mc^2$. To reach this realization, Einstein had to reverse a commonly held view: that time was absolute while the speed of light was variable. By making the speed of light a constant and time relative, Albert Einstein revolutionized the field of physics and paved the way for the atom bomb, particle physics and numerous other discoveries.

Therefore, one of the fundamental anchor points for our Innovation thinking and journey is Albert Einstein's statement, "You can't solve problems with the same level of thinking that created them." His own discoveries were dependent on his ability to build upon the past while also looking beyond its limitations. At Memorial, we accept this challenge to seek out new thinking, new imagination, and new perspectives when we confront difficult problems that vex us and seem to stymie our efforts. Like Einstein, we step back and try a whole new perspective in order to solve problems successfully.[v]

This seems logical and easy to say, but exactly how do we go about gaining new thinking and a fresh perspective on today's organizational problems and challenges? How can Innovation team up with Einstein to help develop creative new products and services or new imaginative solutions?

> *"You can't solve problems with the same level of thinking that created them."*
> ALBERT EINSTEIN

Let us suggest at least three ways that today's successfully innovative organizations are using Einstein's way of thinking to solve their most pressing competitive problems. First, in order to get fresh thinking into their networks to discover imaginative solutions from other industries. Nothing energizes a team more than doing a site visit and seeing a prototype or new offering firsthand and having an opportunity to speak personally to the team members who developed it. Seeing what's possible and learning about the exciting process of development unleashes a team's passion for exploration and discovery. Additionally, such an experience fosters critical new thinking and approaches that can be taken back to the visiting team's organization. Like Einstein, we know to build on rather than disregard our predecessors and peers. Just as he was able to employ disparate theories, we know that getting ideas from outside one's own industry is critical. It removes the rivalry that would undermine a site visit to a potential competitor within the same industry. Also, conventional wisdom and a raft of fixed underlying assumptions and orthodoxies plague all of those within a given industry. Often, a novel idea from a remote field, if modified and applied in a new way, jumpstarts new solutions and a flow of Innovations.

InnoVisit: Whirlpool Corporation

After we were challenged to develop an R&D arm within our organization, our logical next step was to benchmark our industry to see who was already doing this well. Since there were no examples in our own field, we looked to other industries, exploring our own geographic region first since we had no preconceived search tactic. Luckily for us, the headquarters of the Whirlpool Corporation were just a short drive away.

Our Vice President of Marketing and Innovation started by cold-calling the company, that welcomed our interest with enthusiasm. Within weeks we took our first trip, spending about six hours with our hosts. We sat in on staff training sessions, product development discussions, and took a glimpse at the online Innovation pipeline used around the world by Whirlpool staff. Before we left, Whirlpool graciously provided two binders of Innovation policies, procedures, and tools they had collected and refined over many years. They scratched their heads and said they weren't sure how a hospital might use such material, but they gladly shared anyway. In fact, it was only months later that we realized what crucial information this visit had provided. The lessons we learned at Whirlpool jumpstarted our efforts to build a culture of Innovation everywhere at Memorial. Even years later, we refer back to these lessons almost weekly.

We circled back to Whirlpool about seven years after our initial visit and, although the leaders were different, the team members were again kind enough to update us on their work and systems. In addition, they were genuinely interested in all that we had learned along the way. We will be forever grateful for this fortuitous first visit.

Wake-Up Tip:
Jump in with enthusiasm

The second way to use Einstein's novel thinking is to populate your project teams with, as Tom Peters labels them, "freaks, mavericks, and weird thinkers!" Too often we hire, train, and work with people who think, act, and work exactly alike. We engage in group thinking, but since we have similar experiences and perspectives the benefits are limited. People who think differently from most project team members – whether they are labeled freaks, weirdoes, mavericks, free spirits, wild cards or just creative – can help bring a whole new perspective on a current problem and begin to challenge a lot of underlying assumptions and orthodoxies that block our efforts at problem solving and blind us to new and often radically beneficial alternatives and options. We'll introduce you to one of our own "mavericks" later in the book.

Some years ago our CEO was asked to be a "wild card," one of three people chosen from outside the host company's industry to sit in on the organization's strategic planning sessions over a three-day period. He was asked to challenge current thinking, offer fresh new perspectives, and ask questions that went against conventional wisdom of the day. Looking back on it, he recalls, "I hardly considered myself to be weird, freaky, or a maverick," but the company considered his different point of view to be extremely helpful as they planned their future and considered new possibilities and alternatives.

The third way to use Einstein's famous quote is to unleash imagination and creativity through Innovation tools. Brainstorming is the most widely recognized tool, but direct observations, assumption-reversal, alternative futures and unintended consequences are all useful in getting project team members to engage their right brains and their imagination capabilities. Einstein would play his violin or do thought games with his peers. His breakthrough about relativity occurred when walking with a friend. They stood on a rise and considered the speed of light in terms of the distance to various clock towers. Time and light became meshed in Einstein's mind and jumpstarted his new way of thinking. We, too, have learned that new associations and new combinations from different industries often help more analytic, left brained thinkers begin imagining radically new possibilities and options.

What are the consequences of not embracing Einstein's problem solving? First, what you seem to be saying is that you don't need any new thinking and can solve your own problems your own way. Not only is arrogance an organizational learning disability, but it can drive your best talent to other organizations that value new ideas and enjoy being at the forefront of new thinking. Secondly, you also seem to be saying that the smartest dozen people on the planet just happen to work down the hall in your administrative suite, and they are all that's necessary to figure out today's complex problems and global challenges. This type of thinking is at best naïve and at worst the representative of "not made here" reasoning. Either type of thinking can be lethal in a highly competitive market environment. Smart people are everywhere and it helps to network and exchange new ideas with different industries. Why not take advantage of one of the smartest people of all time and introduce new thinking into your Innovation project teams?

Anchor 2: Joseph Juran's Lesson on Improvement

Several decades ago Joseph Juran, one of the founding fathers of the worldwide Quality Improvement movement (along with C. Edwards Deming) stated that, "All improvement comes by way of a project."[vi] This simple statement is a constant reminder that improvement is based in a regular flow of Innovation projects. Why was Dr. Juran so adamant that all improvement was based on the output of a project? Since today's global products and services are the result of hundreds of interdependent processes and systems, they are so complex and multidisciplinary that no one individual or set of individuals could possibly make any significant or lasting improvement without the use of an interdisciplinary improvement project team. If you think this is an overstatement, try making even a small change in your product or service without telling anybody else and see what happens to your e-mail and voice mail systems as one frantic department after another reacts to this surprising change!

"All improvement comes by way of a project."
JOSEPH JURAN

Juran was also arguing for the discipline, structure, and prioritization of an improvement project approach. Projects have definite launchings and endings (no committees here), a defined methodology and leadership, dedicated resources, and agreed-upon milestones along the way. Once launched, the project team follows a rough protocol and methodology and makes use of a variety of tools during the data collection and diagnostic phase of the project. Juran is also building a case for team-based solutions and the use of multidisciplinary teams to bring new thinking and greater insight into the process. Involving actual customers and lead users is critical, especially those from a diverse set of demographics and perspectives. Juran emphasizes that buy-in and the chances of obtaining needed resources are greatly increased when a diverse, broad project team develops solutions and early prototypes.

As Rosabeth Kantor, dean of the Harvard Business School, is fond of saying, "Change is disturbing when it is done to us. Change is exhilarating when it is done by us."[vii] Senior leadership is therefore charged with prioritizing the dozens of project teams ensuring that the entire organization has the opportunity to be involved or contribute to innovation efforts. Being part of the change enriches staff engagement and typically leads to a better outcome. This is also why so many MBA programs devote an entire course on project management; it is how work and problem solving is done in today's highly complex and competitive environment. Organizing and managing dozens of improvement project teams is how today's leaders stay competitive. Whether the project team is improving a quality process, improving a service outcome, or developing a new product or service, projects and project teams are the pulse of today's competitive organizations as they are under pressure to constantly improve all aspects of their products all the time.

Tom Peters, the so-called "father of the modern-day corporation," goes one step further with Juran's concept and adds, "Why not turn an assigned project into a WOW! Project by adding passion, enthusiasm, imagination and creativity until it becomes a cause and something you'll be bragging about for decades." We'll talk more about Tom's WOW! Projects in Chapter 7, but the importance of turning every management assignment or problem-solving project into an Innovation project cannot be stressed enough.

Einstein and Juran help an organization stay firmly anchored in the future, and prevent teams from returning to the old ways of problem-solving and maintaining the status quo or, on the opposite end of the spectrum, from losing hold of the management aspect of Innovation. Essentially, when a new opportunity arises or a nagging problem keeps holding an organization back, the wise Innovation leader immediately asks two questions: "Where are you going to find some new thinking and new solutions to this problem?" and "Have you formed a project team to improve or find a new solution?"

The Next Stage

At this point in our exploration of Innovation, we have covered how to think about and understand the power of the concept, but now we move on to preparatory steps you should take before implementing your Innovation processes. These steps are kept general in order to allow you to integrate them into your own organizational framework.

CHAPTER 3
The Three Plagues

There are three plagues afflicting most organizations today; if left unchecked they will ravage and nearly destroy most of our country's businesses, particularly those in highly competitive industries. These plagues sap the strength, energy, and vitality from an organization and leave the victim in a greatly weakened and vulnerable condition. Until specific Innovation remedies are employed on a broad scale ("the three sanitizers") an organization must remain ever vigilant against these devastating scourges.

Now that you have a team and a focus, let's look at issues may be "plaguing" you. While our experience is primarily with healthcare, these problems are common in many fields and can be addressed by following the methods of Innovation.

We choose the term 'plagues' intentionally, drawing on the lessons learned from the Black Death that took place in Europe in the fourteenth century. No one at the time could be certain what caused the plague or how to stop it, but theories abounded.[viii] In Italy, some scholars believed that to prevent infection one should stay in a positive frame of mind. For example, they advise the afflicted to visit beautiful landscapes and gardens with aromatic plants and listen to melodic music. One can't dismiss these ideas as entirely naïve. After all, the doctors of the time lacked tools as basic as a microscope and were, essentially, working in the dark. The lack of information, modern medicinal techniques, and basic sanitation resulted in the death of a third of Europe's population.

We can translate many of the lessons learned from this period into our organizations today. True, the problems may not be on such a mass, tragic scale, but organizations can be viewed as vulnerable microcosms. The problems we discuss in this chapter can easily spread without proper identification of the cause and careful implementation of an innovative, but effective, cure.

Toxic Creeping Sameness

As you drive to work in the morning, you probably pass several huge billboards advertising the advantages of one heart, cancer, or women's health clinic after another. All hospitals, it seems, have a nationally recognized heart center, the greatest life-saving cancer center, and the most private and caring women's clinic. The hospital radio ads also tell you how up-to-date, technologically sophisticated, and state-of-the-art everyone's center really is. Plus, the night before, there were probably TV commercials on all four major networks about healthcare in your region. This onslaught of marketing makes us shake our heads ruefully. The same advanced equipment these smaller centers are now touting has already been approved a few years ago by our Board of Trustees. Even low-volume centers of questionable quality call themselves the region's leader in heart, cancer, bariatric, orthopedics, or women's services. We may have been ahead of the game, but no one cares about the leader of the first inning, only the ninth.

Like many other industries, healthcare is competitive and focused on distinction through awards. Organizations claim they are #1, the top 100, the top 10, nationally acclaimed, nationally recognized, platinum award winners, or simply the best at a given service. Andy Warhol had it right when he said, "in the future, everyone will be famous for 15 minutes." There seems to be little difference when *everyone* claims to have the best quality, greatest service, largest selection, lowest prices, and best value.

What makes this trend so troubling is that to a more empowered and skeptical public, we are all the same. The real problem for an organization becomes that if the public believes we are so similar, they will treat us all as a basic commodity. A basic commodity has no particularly distinguishing characteristic or quality and, therefore, all buying decisions become, "Who has the lowest price?" If your organization becomes subject to the lowest-price buying decisions, then the future is bleak and capital will flow to other sectors and industries with strong brands and heavily differentiated products and services.

This apparent sameness, as far as consumers are concerned, is also known as the "commoditization trap:" if organizations cannot establish strong brands and great differentiation in key services, the future only holds ever-decreasing prices, fierce competition for dwindling resources, and low access to capital.

The "commoditization trap" especially hurts the high-quality performers because, even though they can produce superior outcomes, there is so much noise in the consumer's advertising channel that people cannot tell one competitor from another. Although word of mouth works well for restaurants, boutiques, and health clubs, the public has little knowledge and often lacks sophistication when comparing one high-technology clinical service against another. Whether you are an award-winning or an award-buying organization, the public is rapidly beginning to think we are all alike and way too costly. In the absence of a strong standout brand, the purchasing decision will focus on price only as the key factor. These are the classic symptoms of the plague of toxic creeping sameness.

It is critical to analyze and diagnose this plague from the customer's point of view and not that of the organization's leadership. Senior management always seems to have a positively biased and entrenched point of view about the quality and "specialness" of its products and services. Often, they can be overheard saying, "If only the public and our customers understood how wonderful our (offering) really is they would…" or "We just need to tell the public that…" These statements are all symptoms of undifferentiated or overly complicated offerings that confuse or fail to meet customer needs.

So what are some cures? Mystery shopping, where you collect data by having researchers pose as consumers, focus groups using ethnographic research, direct observation, and the study of non-users can all yield valuable insights to help offerings avoid toxic creeping sameness. Remember to identify the cause of the plague thoroughly and then use the Innovation methodology to solve it.

In order to use Innovation to differentiate the organization, ensure that you are clear about where Innovation fits into your overall product or services strategy. We often find the integration of a literal goal into a conceptual, visual framework helpful; it gives us our own language of achievement and adds cohesion to a team seeking to achieve a shared goal.

For example, at Memorial we have long adopted the strategy that all of our clinical services should be both getting "better" and being "different" by adding value. These two directions of improvement are illustrated in Figure 5.4 with a USA map superimposed on the chart. Every clinical service should be moving on the horizontal axis to the right by continuously improving its quality. This horizontal axis represents evidence-based medicine, where outcomes are quantified and the principles of quality improvement lead to better outcomes and higher levels of quality. The vertical axis, however, represents the areas where Innovation can help differentiate each clinical service by adding value. Thus, the only way to avoid the plague of toxic creeping sameness is to differentiate every clinical service using continual Innovation as a competitive strategy. Every clinical service needs to keep moving up the differentiation scale as competitors copy, replicate, and develop competing clinical programs and services. The ideal trajectory for any product or service is to move to the upper right on both scales, the northeast quadrant, or as we say at Memorial, "Let's all go to Bar Harbor!" To find your own Bar Harbor, analyze your organization's goals and strongest services. Then create a visual goal or map that represents your plan of achievement through Innovation.

Flesh-Eaten Margins

The best way to understand this plague is to draw from our own experience. Consider the typical hospital. It can be described as having some basic core services surrounded by rings of clinical services and programs each having a different level of profitability. Figure 3.1 shows the basic core set of services: the intensive care rooms, the emergency room, the general medical/surgical beds, and the support services: nursing, housekeeping, nutrition, central supply, etc. The first ring surrounding the core services comprises orthopedics, pediatrics, maternity, neuro/rehab, and mental health; this ring has a greater degree of profitability to the hospital. Even more profitable services occupy the next ring: inpatient radiology, laboratory, cardiac catheterization labs, peripheral vascular labs, and operating rooms. The last ring of services are the most profitable and are largely outpatient-oriented; thus, they are the most easily replicated and moved to other settings. In this ring lie departments such as outpatient radiology, outpatient chemotherapy, outpatient physical therapy, routine laboratory, outpatient surgery, GI lab, and cardiac testing.

Figure 3.1

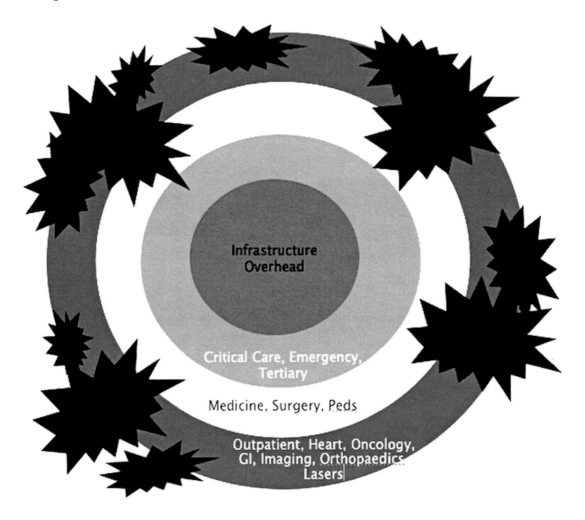

Over the past decade, niche players, entrepreneurial physicians, and for-profit chains have been steadily eating away at these more profitable outer rings of clinical services and programs. Every year as reimbursement tightens, malpractice insurance costs rise, pressure to take hospital emergency calls increases, and physicians' private practice costs skyrocket, hospitals have been steadily seeing their most profitable services pulled out and set up in for-profit outpatient settings. Often called "carve-outs," these bites into profitable services leave the hospital with only the costly core departments. Over one-third of hospitals now operate in the red, and another third barely have any operating margin left. The typical hospital now has a difficult payor mix, ever-tightening reimbursement, rapidly escalating nursing and technologist vacancies, and an aging physical plant. At the same time, capital demands are increasing for more information technology and more clinical technology and an aging physical plant.

Left unchecked, this nibbling away at the profitable services will leave the organization in a weakened and vulnerable condition. Many seek mergers or reduce needed but unprofitable services; however the financial health of most hospitals is deteriorating and the access to needed capital is rapidly being closed off.

On the other hand, a more positive and growing expenditure for this country is discretionary spending for services such as cosmetic surgery, complimentary and integrative medicine, vitamins and nutritional supplements, over-the-counter medicines, and at-home testing kits and equipment. None of these products and services are covered by traditional health insurance, and the public is increasingly willing to pay for them out of their own pockets. There are two large and important groups driving this rise in discretionary spending: baby boomers and health and fitness enthusiasts. Both groups will spend an increasing percentage of their income to stay healthy, look young, and lead active, fit lifestyles.

However, hospitals limit their involvement in this huge flow of discretionary spending and, in fact, only seem interested in offering what government and third party payors reimburse. This "reimbursement mentality" blinds organizations from even seeing services that are highly profitable and are only covered by out-of-pocket spending. Consequently, entrepreneurs, niche players, and national for-profit retailers have moved in and captured almost every one of these services, again leaving the hospitals with expensive, low-margin services and safety-net programs. Many newer technologies for cosmetic surgery or physical fitness are introduced and discussed at non-healthcare trade shows or professional society meetings where no hospital representatives are ever present, and where more entrepreneurial physicians can pick which ones they get to own (especially when they are first introduced and the profit margins are highest).

All this brings us back to Leland Kaiser's question — our wake-up call. Why don't hospitals have their own R&D policies? Hospitals have a rich flow of new technology, new pharmaceuticals, and new information technology. It's not that hospitals don't have access to the output of thousands of research and development departments each year. It's simply that hospitals themselves don't have an R&D budget of their own to help reinvent their future and design new capabilities for their own benefit. This is true for many organizations, not just hospitals. The R&D spending and flow of technologies always come from vendors, suppliers, and for-profit organizations on their terms and within their time frames, channels of distribution, and profit motives. Without an R&D policy and budget, an organization has no real way to experiment or prototype new delivery systems, new customer care models, or new products or services. Organizations in this position need a way to tap into the incredible amounts of intellectual capital they and their staff possess. Only then can new dollars flow into Innovations that the organizations partially own or for which they receive compensation.

So what is the sanitizer for the plague of flesh-eaten margins? Diagnostics are easy to implement by examining where margins are really coming from and for how long. 3M has pioneered the "X% of new profits coming from new products/services that were developed within the past Y years" approach, a potentially sobering way to analyze long term, undifferentiated offerings. Be careful not to confuse minor improvements in small features and benefits with new innovative and creative offerings that attract or delight customers in brand new ways. A thorough examination of the barriers to entry by new niche players and entrepreneurs is also necessary to assess the long-term viability of current margins and likely profitability. Low barriers mean a need for a large and full pipeline of new offerings that keep your products fresh, cutting-edge, and highly resistant to imitation. Finally, an analysis of key customer assumptions is needed to challenge the status quo. The Build-a-Bear Company has grown to offer much more than their original Teddy Bear experience. The company also analyzes customer assumptions on a daily basis through their online community where kids can provide direct feedback to the company CEO. If these assumptions were to change dramatically, they would either produce huge opportunities or wreck your business model entirely. Customer assumptions are often hidden, subconscious, and tricky to examine on a regular basis. To return to Einstein and Tom Peters' ideas, it may require someone from outside the industry to probe, challenge, and unearth these orthodoxies, mental models, and underlying assumptions.

Leaking Talent

Why does *Fortune Magazine* spend so much time and effort creating a list of the best places to work each year? Why are companies so desirous of being on that list? After all, the places deemed great to work at offer expensive perks seeming to undermine profit margins. The answer is simple: the happier your team, the better they will be. The more people want to work for you, the more qualified your applicants and employees will be. In our case, we strive to create a great place to work so that we can provide our patients with advanced care by excellent providers. Plus, employee retention makes economic sense: turnover results in higher new employee training expenses. As we foresee a future where nurses are in increasingly short supply, we endeavor to improve our corporation so that we will always attract the best of those available. We must create exceptional working environments and fabulous cultures if we hope to attract and retain the best and brightest workforce for the future.

Successful organizations need great team members, not just good ones. And creating a work environment doesn't simply mean installing in-house saunas and mini-golf courses in the cafeteria. Star performers want to know they are part of something meaningful, that their efforts make a difference for their company, their industry, and the world. This kind of engaged employee is passionate to do great work.

We've learned that a culture of Innovation is inspiring and can enhance efforts to attract and retain the best. It's increasingly important to talented professionals to work where their ideas are valued and to remain on the leading edge of their field. Stagnant cultures, mountains of unproductive paperwork, and command-and-control styles of management all work to drive out the best talent and leave behind those with the least skills, mobility, and options.

Again, the diagnostics show that asking staff for ideas in a non-threatening and blame-free way encourages them to participate in the implementation of their suggestions and to see how open to new ideas the organization's leaders really are. Gauging the culture surrounding new ideas and new thinking is also key; creating metrics for the number of new ideas implemented in X months, or the number of staff who actively work on exploring and implementing new ideas, is critical to monitoring progress as well as spotting bottlenecks and idea-killing leaders.

Along with the common sense rule that you should never shop when hungry, there is also the rule that you should never shop without a list. It keeps you on track. Listing these plagues serves the same purpose. You have a clear idea of both the positive and negative aspects of your organization. You know what Innovation means and what you want it to help you achieve. Now you need ideas that will address the three plagues. These ideas will come from your own people, but as we've discussed, outside input should always be welcome. Where do you begin? As with all good puzzles, it's best to start with the corners.

---

[i]   Roger L. Martin, *The Design of Business* (Boston, MA: Harvard Business Press, 2009).

[ii] Larry Keeley, *Types of Innovation*.

[iii] Daniel H. Pink. *A Whole New Mind.* (New York: Riverhead Books, 2005).

[iv] Bodanis, David, *E=MC²* (Berkley, CA: Berkley Press, 2001).

[v]   Gary Hamel, *Leading the Revolution: How to Thrive in Turbulent Times by Making Innovation a Way of Life* (Boston, MA: Harvard Business Press, 2002).

[vi] J.M. Juran, *Juran on Leadership for Quality* (New York, NY: Free Press, 2003), 35.

[vii] Rosabeth Kantor

[viii] Knox, E.L. Skip, "The Black Death," *The History of Western Civilization* (Boise State University, www.BoiseState.edu), 1-2.

CHAPTER 4

The Four Corners

Learning how and where to innovate in your organization may seem much like putting together a jigsaw puzzle with many pieces. You should adopt this metaphor right from the beginning and begin to fit some pieces together, following the golden rule of puzzles: start with the four corners.

As your senior leaders begin the seemingly mysterious journey toward learning about Innovation, the thought of actually organizing and applying these new principles and lessons may seem overwhelming. You may feel overwhelmed by the expansive control panel of the plane you are learning to fly. As you see others head down the runway on either side, you may also feel like a late starter in the increasingly popular and successful endeavor. Honestly, you may also be coming from an industry that was not in the habit of reinventing its future proactively, but rather relied on outside vendors and suppliers to introduce new technology, products, and services. Disconcerting though this may be, push your fears aside; you will stand out because of your enthusiasm, excitement, courage, passion, and long-term commitment.

As you begin to explore the ideas of Innovation, you may feel much as though you are putting together a jigsaw puzzle with many pieces. You will soon learn there is no picture on the box to guide your efforts! This is both liberating and frightening.

On the one hand, it lets you design your own goal, but it also raises your anxiety levels, especially for those used to step-by-step instructions and well-worn, familiar techniques. You should take a breath and begin to fit some pieces together much as any puzzle solver would: by starting with the four corner pieces.

Corner 1: Identify the Core Group and Champions

An early question that often arises is, "Who in our organization is best to help head up the Innovation revolution?" After all, you shouldn't go alone. First, identify the initial core leaders to help you.

We have a proven way to identify not just those capable of Innovation, but also those ready to take a leadership role. This technique works every time, in any size organization, in any industry. Just send out six Innovation articles from *Fast Company, Inc., Entrepreneur,* or *HBR* to about 20 – 25 people in your organization. When looking for the first group to form, it's not about balancing all areas of the company. Start by looking for those with an active right brain, those who have high energy and an obvious passion for their work. These types of contributors will help advance the new thinking since it compliments how they've been approaching their work naturally. Announce that this informal, ad-hoc group will be meeting each week for six straight weeks to review one of the articles. Anyone who is interested in discussing these articles should meet at Starbucks at 7:00 a.m. on the next six Tuesday mornings. At the end of six weeks, there will be a handful of excited, enthusiastic, passionate leaders whose "hair is on fire" about Innovation and the opportunities ahead. They are committed, knowledgeable, and proven early risers.

This core group, since they self-selected as proponents of the movement, are the foundation around which you can build your change efforts. They can't wait to get started, they come from all over your enterprise, and once released will never be content to preserve the status quo or say "just good enough."

Next, you need to work with the team to expand your base and identify champions. To get started, we selected several assessment instruments to provide an indication of Innovation capacity in an individual. The Hartman Value Profile[1] (HVP) and the Bar-On Emotional Quotient Inventory[2] (EQ-i) gave us some insights into an individual's capacity to be innovative. The HVP assesses Innovation potential by describing Innovation as a unique manifestation of an individual's human judgment capacity. The EQ-i profiled the CEOs of the Young Presidents' Organization (YPO) and the Innovator's Alliance (IA) and found that these CEOs score high in several emotional intelligence skill sets. These skill sets align with the implications described in the HVP.

Based on this research, we identified eight human characteristics important to one's capacity for innovation:

1. Intuitive sensitivity and empathy. (HVP, EQ-i)
2. Creative problem solving skills. (HVP, EQ-i)
3. Appreciation of big-picture perspectives and optimism. (HVP, EQ-i)
4. Adaptability and comfort with change. (HVP, EQ-i)
5. Ability to discern important issues and control impulses. (HVP, EQ-i)
6. Assertiveness (HVP, EQ-i)
7. Capacity to deal with difficult situations and interpersonal relationships. (HVP, EQ-i)
8. Stress tolerance (HVP, EQ-i)

All managers at Memorial complete a series of leadership assessments (including the HVP and EQ-I) that provide feedback on the four imperatives of leadership as well as their Innovation capacity. Like A.G. Lalley[3], CEO of P & G, we believe that making "Innovation work is the job of leadership." Therefore, a leadership profile (Figure 4.1) is created for each manager. This allows us not only to identify individuals who currently have a higher likelihood or capacity to be innovative, but also to assist others in improving their capacity. As we said earlier, we often partner those who tested lower or have little experience with individuals having a high Innovation presence or a clear Innovation capacity according to assessments and proven experience on projects.

To make clear the importance of the eight Innovation characteristics, we should explain how each one impacts a person's ability to innovate.

Figure 4.1

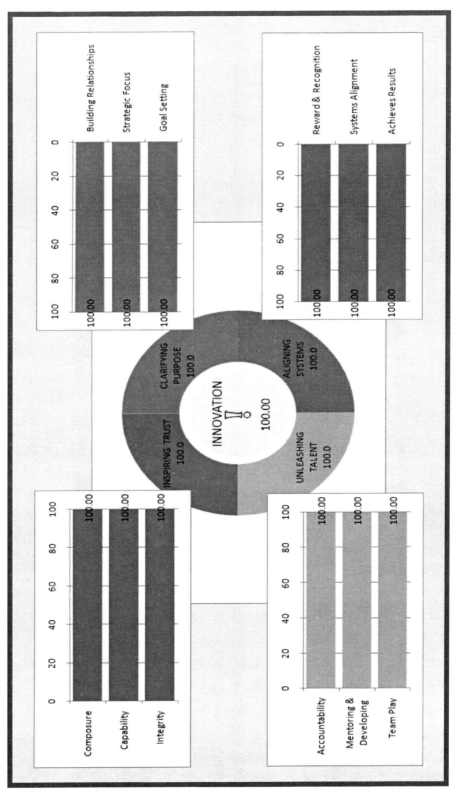

INTUITIVE SENSITIVITY AND EMPATHY

Intuitive sensitivity describes a person's ability to look beyond the obvious facts of the matter. When a person becomes focused on a particular task or assignment, there is a tendency to overlook other possibilities or alternatives. HVP aims to measure the ability to be more insightful, a primary component of Innovation. Empathy is closely related to intuitive sensitivity. Empathy is the ability to be aware of, to understand, and to appreciate the feelings and thoughts of others. In his book *Wired to Care*, Dev Patniak, president of Jump, points out the incredible advances in product and service growth experienced by companies who were tuned-in to the customers. Patniak goes on to say that when you step outside of yourself, you open up to the possibility of seeing new opportunities to connect with the customer. Being empathic also shifts an adversarial relationship to a collaborative relationship where new learning and synergy can exist.

CREATIVE PROBLEM SOLVING

Creative, efficient problem-solving and confident decision-making are critical ingredients in Innovation. These traits encompass a person's capacity to see what is relevant in complex situations, and to experience and process broad spectrums of information in such a way that new possibilities emerge. Creative problem-solving often requires looking at a situation from different perspectives. Clearly, empathy is also an important ingredient in creative problem solving.

APPRECIATES BIG-PICTURE PERSPECTIVES AND OPTIMISM

The ability to see issues from a big-picture point of view allows an individual to see more possibilities and options than individuals who lack this perspective. With optimism, one can continue looking for plausible alternatives in difficult and challenging times. Coming up with new and innovative solutions requires accepting failure as an important part of the journey. Continually looking for the next right answer instead of taking a broader view leaves little hope for achieving or sustaining Innovation.

ADAPTABILITY AND COMFORT WITH CHANGE

Innovators are change agents who are decidedly dissatisfied with comfort zones and protecting the status quo. They tend to be agile, synergistic, and capable of reacting to change, without rigidity. They are open to and appreciative of different ideas, orientations, ways, and practices.

ABILITY TO DISCERN IMPORTANT ISSUES AND CONTROL IMPULSES

The ability to discern issues of importance and observe the connections among events without getting caught up in the urgency to resolve everything is a key skill of innovators. Through strong impulse control, an innovative individual is able to take the necessary time to discover and explore alternative possibilities.

ASSERTIVENESS

The most effective innovators will be assertive about their ideas and convictions. They are passionate about finding the next right answer. Whereas they usually seek first to understand additional insights and information, they are also eager to share their opinions and ideas in a respectful way. They feel confident in themselves and engage in dialogue with honesty and a deep desire to seek new and better alternatives.

CAPACITY TO DEAL WITH DIFFICULT SITUATIONS AND INTERPERSONAL RELATIONSHIPS

Since new ideas and insights are often the result of challenging, robust discussion with a diverse team, all of those involved must function in a positive and respectful manner if progress is to be achieved. Strong interpersonal skills are critical for creating a safe environment that allows free and open sharing of ideas and thoughts.

STRESS TOLERANCE

Stress has been shown at the HeartMath Institute[5] to interfere with the body's ability to engage the brain in higher levels of thinking and performance. A person's ability to manage stress in a positive and effective manner is critical to creating an environment where Innovation can prevail.

If your organization isn't yet in a position to implement the HVP and EQ-i assessments, consider the characteristics objectively: utilize your human resources department or personal knowledge of your team to determine initial champions and project team members. This process has the added advantage of kick-starting your corporation's internal awareness of Innovation.

Two common disciplines that have a natural connection to the benefits of Innovation are marketing and information technology. Those in marketing appreciate the importance of differentiation when making a message or brand stand out from the competition. Those in information technology are already comfortable with the constant change that is an integral part of their field.

Along with assessment of human resources, research and reading likewise play a significant role in getting started with an Innovation revolution. As previously mentioned, the magazine Fast Company rapidly became the centerpiece of our Innovation discussions, and we went back and re-read every issue cover to cover to begin distilling some key lessons and establishing early principles and objectives. Other magazines such as Red Herring, Entrepreneur, Inc., Success, and Harvard Business Review were also useful to the core group, especially those from the world of high tech, business start-ups, and the entertainment/amusement industries. Likewise, a library of books (nearly a hundred) was established covering the broad topics of Innovation, creativity, entrepreneurship, inventorship, project management, transformational leadership, and hightech industries.[1] Our Innovation Propulsion Lab (see Chapter 6) was encouraged to read one new book each month and share key insights, learning the practical applications. (To see our complete book list, view the Appendix.)

Corner 2: InnoVisits to Innovation Mentors

We've already told you about some of the mentors and Innovative companies with whom we now have relationships. We waited until this point to offer a complete explanation of InnoVisits because in order for them to be useful, you must have a clear idea of your culture and goals before you go. Also, create your own list of questions prior to the visit in order to keep it focused and productive. On our early InnoVisits numerous questions and issues surfaced: How do you get organized and staffed for

---

[1] Authors who were particularly helpful and insightful were Tom Peters' *The Circle of Innovation, WOW! Projects, the Project 50*, and *Reimagine*; Gary Hamel's two books; Gilmore and Pine's *The Experience Economy*; and Larry Keeley of Monitor Doblin's *The Power of Innovation* (VHA).

Innovation? What tools were useful and what processes to follow? Should just a few with already-demonstrated creative skills be involved, or should the movement be broader? What rewards and recognitions are effective? How should teams best access resources to begin? Where should an organization first focus its effort? How should risk and failure be evaluated and measured? We had to learn on the go, but we encourage you to study our experience in order to prepare. To get you started, we've included The 21 Steps InnoVisit Checklist for Smarties in the Appendix, as well as an InnoVisit idea capture tool to bring back key insights, new findings, and critical follow-up for future networking.

When you go, take along a team – board of governance members, key customers, and other Csuite senior leaders in order to build support and provide the broadest base of learning possible. As our friends from Nike would say, "Just Do It." With this team, these questions, and lots of blank paper, off we went to learn.

How did we start and whom did we choose to visit? There were a few different types of organizations: large companies and organizations, research universities, and venture capitalists. Since we were looking beyond our own field, we chose not to limit our mentors to one specific type of organization; rather, we took advantage of the insights offered by all of them.

Who should you visit?

❏ Innovative Companies and Organizations

❏ Research Universities

❏ Venture Capitalists

Also, have you been hearing one name over and over again? That was the case with us; we kept hearing about IDEO again and again. After our InnoVisit to IDEO, we certainly knew why. Similarly, you should consider contacting an organization that pops up on your radar more than three times.

INNOVATIVE COMPANIES AND ORGANIZATIONS

When many organizations, especially those in manufacturing, first became interested in continuous quality improvement (CQI) or total quality management (TQM) back in the late 1980's and early 1990's, the prevailing wisdom was to go on site visits to the great companies that were known for superior quality: Florida Power and Light, Motorola, Milliken, Xerox, and IBM. You should apply the same lessons to planning InnoVisits, by selecting companies with a solid track record of Innovation for decades, who depend on a regular flow of innovative products and services, and who would agree to spend hours with a "just-beginning-the-adventure" visiting leadership team.

As scary and awkward as this might seem at first, after about three to four InnoVisits an interesting shift begins to take place. Start with companies where you may already have a relationship, such as those in your supplier base. Do some research on their current activities and contact the inventor behind the coolest product they have on the market. Avoid the sales department since you're more interested in learning than buying at this point.

After a few of our InnoVisits, the companies hosting us became increasingly interested in us and in our organizational education from the Innovation processes we studied. After seven or eight InnoVisits, we were offering to our hosts as many insights and new models as they were sharing with us. After all, most of these wildly innovative organizations don't research other companies as we did, and we found more than a hint of envy for our band of naïve, ever-questioning teammates who never seemed to tire of learning new thinking and new challenges.

InnoVisit: Baxter Corporation

In 2003, we visited Baxter Corporation in suburban Chicago. Baxter happened to be one of our medical supply vendors, but we were certainly not one of their biggest customers. Still, our request to meet their Innovation team was welcomed. On the day of the visit we were surprised to see five to six executives on hand to welcome us into a full agenda about Innovation. We were even scheduled to meet with Harry Kramer, Baxter's president and CEO at the time.

When Harry Kramer entered the room the energy level quadrupled and he seemed genuinely pleased to meet us and curious about why a hospital of any size would be researching Innovation strategies. Our CEO explained our belief that building an Innovation culture would prepare us for almost anything, and Kramer seemed to like what we had to say. He shared his ideas openly and then kindly offered the full resources of Baxter's Innovation team to assist us in any way they could. He did ask if we would kindly add 30 minutes to the end of our visit so they could share some information about a new product they would be launching, and of course we agreed.

At the end of our formal session, the Baxter team members seemed to get a glimmer in their eyes. A staff member entered the boardroom and distributed sample bottles of a beverage we had never seen before. The team explained that in a few weeks Baxter Corporation would be launching its first consumer product: the Pulse Health drinks we were currently taste testing. They explained the top secret planning and the test city schedule. As we asked them questions about the formulas, bottles, and marketing, the discussion quickly turned toward ways hospitals, and especially our hospital, could assist in the launch.

By the end of our session, we had some ideas flowing and within about four months, Memorial became the first hospital in the country to have its own privately labeled family of health drinks. This was one of our first strategic alliances through the Memorial Venture Center, and it was unexpected but informative. While we did receive modest revenues through internal distribution, what was more important was the inside knowledge we gained about how new products get to market, how companies deal with decision-making in uncharted territory, and how we could bring value to billion-dollar companies as a test-bed organization.

Thereafter, we had bold plans for ways to use the Pulse drinks; however, another company acquired the Pulse line within two years and our connection did not carry over. Our connection with Baxter continues and we certainly benefited from their expertise and knowledge. This experience gave us the thirst (no pun intended) for more alliances, building our knowledge base and pool of friends.

Wake-Up Tip:
Gather experience everywhere.

RESEARCH UNIVERSITIES

Our experience in doing InnoVisits to nationally recognized research universities has been extremely helpful. Should you pursue this route, there are two places to visit, one pretty much unknown and the other fairly obvious. The first place to visit is the little known Office of Technology Transfer. This office is responsible for taking the intellectual property of the faculty and its research base and converting that into a revenue stream through patents, licenses, copyrights, and commercial applications. At first, you may wonder how this fits into your Innovation strategy or your existing business. The idea here is that your employee base and your organizational networks all constitute a huge and valuable intellectual property pool that has great revenue potential if organized and wired correctly. The Tech Transfer Offices we visited all shared their processes for capturing this intellectual capital and converting it into a wide variety of commercial ventures. This is an extremely valuable skill set to develop and grow for future ventures. All the Tech Transfer Offices offered business planning and mentoring programs, assistance in writing a business plan, coaching through various stages of development, and some seed funding.

One Innovation leader shared with us the four 'I's, necessary steps in this commercialization process. First is the "Insight" which makes people aware of the value and function of the Tech Transfer Office and how and why to access its many strategic services. Likewise, staff in the Office were also highly engaged with the research projects and publishing of the faculty so they could spread awareness of intellectual capital. The next 'I' is "Innovate," the act of taking the good ideas moving them to market. Research is conducted on the size of markets, emerging customer or end-user needs, and national trends. The "Infrastructure" phase provides buildings, wet labs, programming business planning, and research assistants to begin the prototyping and commercialization phases. Finally, the "Incubation" phase involves start-up assistance, seed capital, financing, mentoring, and business partnering. Often, graduate students are employed to assist with these phases and, of course, the university has a strict revenue-sharing formula between the faculty, department, research lab and university.

The next stop on your InnoVisit will be to the business school, specifically the director and faculty of the entrepreneurship program/department. This is one of the hot, growing areas of concentration, and this talented faculty is more than happy to share their curriculum, their reading lists and books, and overall experiences in teaching at the undergraduate, graduate, and executive levels. Many sponsor business plan competitions that are often open to the public or those expressing interest. Since Innovation shares so much in common with entrepreneurship (or intrapreneurship), the Business Schools offer a high caliber of speakers, advice, and counsel, and a pool of graduate students who can be employed on many Innovation projects around your organization.

VENTURE CAPITALISTS

One of the many surprises in our journey has been the interesting and exciting people often involved in Innovation and business start-ups. The visits with venture capitalists (VC's) and the entrepreneurship programs help teach the process of starting a business from scratch, often with little or no funding (bootstrapping), and growing it to a size that leads to an exit strategy (being acquired by a large company, a merger, or going public). Irrespective of your organization's size and financial strength, R&D projects often have to start out on a shoestring budget with little assistance to the struggling entrepreneur (or intrapreneur).

The venture capitalists we met (and there were dozens of them) were accustomed to seeing hundreds of ideas and business plans every year and had great expertise in sorting out those with promise from those that had an uncertain future. Since most of us in any industry are lucky to see a few good ideas or business plans in our entire careers, it is helpful to have a group of experts who see so many and can teach you how to sort through them effectively. This is an especially valuable skill for any organization that is interested in growing new businesses, developing a venture center, or fostering entrepreneurs.

Venture capitalists' second most valuable skill is their ability to evaluate the Innovation champion and team. There is an old question in the VC world, that if you had an A player with a B idea or a B player with an A idea, which one would you bet on? The experienced VC's all bet on the A player, the one with the smarts, guts, and patience to steer a good idea all the way to commercial success, even though the odds against him or her are substantial, and the hurdles and barriers might seem daunting. VC's can spot these winners better than nearly anybody and can help share what qualities they look for and how they evaluate great entrepreneurial talent.

The VC's have also had a great deal of time on their hands the last few years due to the low number of business start-ups, a lack of IPOs, and a difficult recession. Consequently, many are more than willing to serve as speakers, provide valuable advice on business ventures, review term sheets, and serve as a sounding board for ideas and emerging trends. VC's are after great ideas in all fields, but especially the life sciences. They also want to identify entrepreneurs and champions. Try to carve out time to network with them and include them at your seminars, Innovation training classes, and exposure to your best and brightest dreamers. This is really an important corner of the puzzle that can have long-term benefits and greatly increase your chances for real success.

The key to InnoVisits, of course, is asking meaningful questions of insightful and helpful experts. Only after several site visits, endless reading, and purposeful networking will curious organizations begin to grasp the basics of Innovation and how to organize for it. Every time you go out, your questions will become deeper and more insightful. You will have different models, principles, and practices to compare and contrast and you will find the key leverage points and successful models to apply to your culture. You learn by doing, not by just talking. So firsthand experience with good guidance, counsel, and advice are a necessary foundation.

Corner 3: Discover Innovation Types

Often, the key to a successful Innovation program is finding the area in which your organization should focus. Look at your field and compare it to the range of Innovation options, such as Larry Keeley and Doblin's "10 Types of Innovation," which fall into a series of categories: finance, process, offering, and delivery. These categories address ways to differentiate your organization outside inventing a new product. See the list below for the complete spectrum.

- FINANCE
  → Business model –Examine how your organization makes money. How could it be better?
  → Networking – This relates not only to your structure and value chain but also to any partnerships with other organizations or groups.
- PROCESS
  → Enabling – These are the processes or capabilities you can purchase from others that improve your capacities and/or efficiency.
  → Core – These proprietary processes add value to your organization.
- OFFERING
  → Product performance – Improve the essential features, performance, or functionality of your product.
  → Product system – This relates to improvements in the support structure

for your offering.

→ Service – How do you support your customers?

• DELIVERY

→ Channel – How do you link your customers to your product and services?

→ Brand – What makes your product and organization identifiable? How do your customers recognize your benefits and ideas?

→ Customer experience – How do you create an integrated experience for your customers? See Chapter 7 for more information on how to do this.

What does your field look like in terms of these areas of differentiation? Are there any gaps – places where you and your competitors have traditionally never focused? Consider making one of these gaps an Innovation Platform for your organization (see Chapter 6). Doblin worked with us on how to use the chart below to identify the core areas where teams can consider focusing their innovation energy.

Finance		Process	
Business model	Networking	Enabling process	Core process

Offering			Delivery		
Product performance	Product system	Service	Channel	Brand	Customer experience

Corner 4: Innovation Vision, Mission, and Intent

The fourth corner of the Innovation puzzle concerns an organization's forward movement. Based on the analysis and diagnostics your organization will have built a strong case for moving beyond the status quo. Therefore, you need to begin the arduous process of imagining a brighter, more compelling future. There are a few components that are critical to articulating the transformation process. Each one requires an enlightened team effort to help build the Innovation competency within the broader organization's culture, and therefore greatly amplifies the chances for success.

INNOVATION VISION

Our visions of the future of our company, products or services tap into our creative power and reflect what we care about most. They often provide form and expression to our aspirations. They are a rich source of models, images, and frameworks for answering an organization's fundamental question, i.e., "What do we want to create?" Leland Kaiser points out that what we envision must express our deepest values and principles. If we are to create our own future rather than remaining passive. Visioning generates images of possibility and high potential, and is best done by enlightened leadership in a group creation approach.

Linda Marks, an author of *Living with Vision*[i], believes that just as everyone has the capacity to innovate, everyone has the power to vision. It is a creative power that often expresses our most desired possibilities. According to Marks, a vision evokes and makes use of multi-sensory expressions, as well as often stories and myths.

We need a powerful vision to provide stability and anchor us in the future, especially when we venture into unfamiliar and unknown areas of Innovation. Visioning brings out our fullest potential as we consider all our talents, dreams and worthy aspirations. Not only does a vision offer hope and possibility, but when everything seems to be so quickly changing and global in scale, it provides a focus and rallying point for our lives. Visions also afford a long-term view of organizational life and provide a fixed star by which to steer in a new direction.

Dan Beckham, a strategic thinker in healthcare over the past few decades, warns that vision statements usually take" at least a paragraph to achieve sufficient specificity and direction. And that paragraph should be built out of simple words. It should be "a clear argument for worthy aspirations. Clarity trumps inspiration." The vision statement should provide a clear sense of where you are going but also of what you won't do. It then becomes an allocator of scarce resources and serves as a bright light to steer you through unchartered possibilities. Beckham also recommends that your vision statement change every 3 – 5 years so that it provides a consistent narrative for everyone in the organization.

INNOVATION INTENT

One of the most important habits, according to Stephen Covey's *7 Habits of Highly Effective People*, is to "begin with the end in mind."[ii] This keeps you focused on the core of what you intend to have happen, what you aspire to create. Throughout our learning about Innovation, we focused on strengthening our organization for long-term viability. At the beginning, we didn't know what diverse paths would develop, but we committed to remaining a relevant organization, disallowing our efforts to be mediocre.

Lastly, of all the early skills acquired, nothing is more important than enthusiastically cultivating your Innovation network of individuals, organizations, and leaders from around the country. Keep your networking partners and colleagues up-to-date on your efforts, share interesting lessons with everyone, and help others share information and knowledge. This is crucial to your early success and one of the most important and vital pieces of your growing intellectual capital.

Enthusiasm, excitement, and a genuine willingness to share insights are the hallmarks of great networking and one of the keys to early success. In fact, at Memorial we found great benefits when we moved from "networking" to "netweaving." This is where we become the matchmaker from one group to another, constantly looking for ways to achieve win-win connections among our new friends.

Even after the four corners of Innovation are set, all leaders should continue to work on other pieces of the puzzle regarding networking, InnoVisits, journal clubs, and new alliances well into the future. There are always new insights to learn and new partnerships to form that help you achieve your Innovation objectives. As an increasing number of organizations discover new methods, we will all be in better control of our preferred futures.

[i]   Linda Marks. *Living With Vision: Reclaiming the Power of the Heart* (Houston, Texas: Knowledge Systems, Inc., now Halliburton, 1989).

[ii]   Stephen Covey, *7 Habits of Highly Effective People* (New York, NY: Free Press, 2004)

Five Essential Lessons

After many InnoVisits, much reading, and lots of networking, a bright light bulb suddenly illuminated our path and provided clarity and foresight.

The ancient Greek philosopher Heraclitus famously said, "You can never step into the same river twice." This certainly applies to the constantly changing business environment, with its rapid diffusion of technology, shifting consumer patterns, and relentless government regulation. These and other factors keep the waters stirred up and continually change its clarity and flow. However, after studying Innovation over a number of years, InnoVisiting and networking with dozens of organizations and experts, the rapidly moving waters of Innovation cleared substantially. Now, we still may not have the clarity a Caribbean coast snorkeler enjoys, but five lessons have emerged that helped us organize our organization for the long journey toward Everyday Innovation and Innovation Everywhere.

These are the five essential ideas we've learned through our research, reflection and experience over the past 15 years. Does this mean everyone agrees that these are the only five lessons required? No, but these are the key insights necessary to begin crafting an Innovation strategy, organizing an implementation schedule, and getting real experience with services, programs, and products. This is where you are — ready to roll up your sleeves and tighten the nuts and bolts on the aircraft before getting Innovation off the ground in your specific organization. As with all information in this book, we just provide the runway and trust that you will do amazing things over the next several years through your additional experience, ongoing site visits, and networking.

Lesson 1: The "Great Man" Theory
Versus the "Everyone Model"

Early on, we learned that the Innovation movement was advancing beyond the longheld "Great Man" theory. This older theory was predicated on the belief that there were a special few who possessed certain creative skills, who seemed to be wired differently than most others, and who could produce a regular flow of great ideas and inventions. After all, weren't Thomas Edison, Albert Einstein, and the thousands of scientists, engineers, and computer specialists working in research labs a special breed of people who possessed superior skills, greater intellect, and broader visions of what's possible? Even in this book, we've highlighted Einstein, Juran, and other thinkers on Innovation in order to explain theories and ideas. Plus, having brilliant people in research and development labs is crucial for Innovation and rapid improvement of technologies.

However, there is a problem. This "Great Man" theory rests on the premise that only a select few are creative and can help innovate, while the rest of the population has little aptitude for After many InnoVisits, much reading, and lots of networking, a bright light bulb suddenly illuminated our path and provided clarity and foresight. A flow of ongoing daily creativity. We just explained in the last chapter that this is untrue, that Innovation can be developed and cultivated. Many others agree. In fact, most companies have moved away from the "Great Man" theory because it excludes 99 percent of their workforce. In addition, it makes the fatal assumption that the very consumers who are the target audience for our products and services are incapable of appreciating the innovative products developed by a select "great" few.

Instead, a second theory now predominates: everyone has some ability to be creative, and everyday people (including our own employees) can have key insights and make important connections that lead to great Innovations and a powerful set of ideas. Strategos, the Innovation consulting company led by Innovation guru

Gary Hamel, leads the pack in taking advantage of these potential Innovators. For example, at whirlpool we found when we visited that every employee has the ability to participate by contacting one of the hundreds of innovation mentors trained to help people use their innovation process to develop ideas. The inclusion of all employees in the Innovation process is a natural outgrowth for companies with a positive, supportive culture. There may be certain individuals in the organization who initially possess a more developed Innovation Presence; however, issuing an inclusive statement that everyone interested is welcome to participate in generating and implementing new ideas can be a powerful way to develop your organization's morale and values.

Doblin, a leading Innovation strategy firm, sees a related distinction between what they call the Creativity and Discipline schools of thought. The Creativity School believes that Innovation occurs most often and best when creative people get together in creative spaces, use creative tools and exercises, and dress and act in creative ways. This allows them to generate new ideas, insights, connections, and wild and crazy suggestions during a so-called "Ideation" phase or process. Underlying the Creativity School's approach is an implicit belief in a channeling or "great funnel" style of Innovation:

Figure 5.1: The Great Funnel Approach

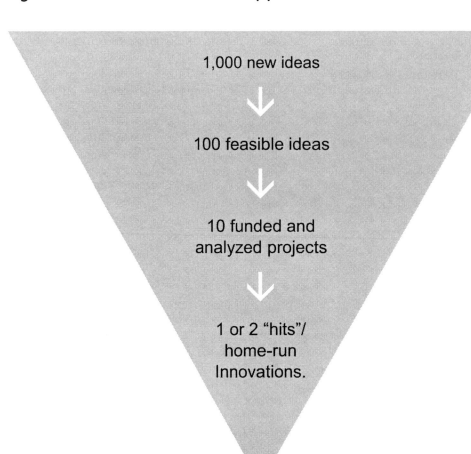

1,000 new ideas

↓

100 feasible ideas

↓

10 funded and
analyzed projects

↓

1 or 2 "hits"/
home-run
Innovations.

Lesson 2: Innovation is a messy, sloppy, irrational, non-linear, unpredictable process

Graph 5.2

One way to visualize the differences between "business as usual" projects and Innovation projects is to compare the respective *pro formas* we often show our Boards for approvals to make internal funding decisions. In both the hospital and in university business plan competitions, these *pro formas* generally resemble a "hockey stick" shape. The projects typically lose money for two or three years and then magically turn around after year three and take an ever-upward path to uninterrupted profitability thereafter (see graph 5.1). These are so common that most of the business plan competition judges report an endless parade hockey stick *pro formas* from nearly all the entrants, with little insight into wildly shifting competitors, disruptive new technologies that can emerge, and new entrants from outside the typical markets.

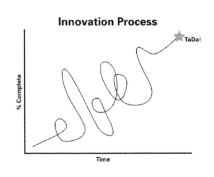

The progress of Innovation, on the other hand, hardly resembles a hockey stick; rather, it seems full of twists, turns, restarts, blind alleys, unproductive cul-de-sacs, and unpredictable events (see graph 5.2). Senior leadership teams who are comfortable with this sloppy, messy process are rare indeed, but the twists and turns are essential to the long-term success of an organization's Innovation efforts.

Nearly everyone in the field agrees that Innovation is not a neat, tightly controlled, linear process that lends itself to tidy charts and easily recognizable milestones. Innovation comes from the oddest places, in the most unusual forms, and from the intersections of strange and distant disciplines. After having studied Innovation for many years, Tom Peters reminds us that it almost always seems to come from "the wrong person, in the wrong place, in the wrong industry, at the wrong time, for the wrong reasons."[1] Additionally, Peters reminds us that when an Innovation team looks back at the extremely messy, sloppy, start-and-stop, redefine, redesign, reinvent process of taking a great idea all the way to a commercially viable product or service, the team almost always says, "Ye gads! Any group of idiots could do a better job of managing a process than that. Next time, let's get organized and cut the mistakes down by 80 percent and the time in half!" Tom Peters claims that "within the 'let's get organized next time' statement lies the kiss of death because the messy, sloppy, unpredictable process requires you to make dozens (hundreds) of mistakes every time you try to innovate or bring something new and exciting to the market!"

Likewise, Innovation is often at the intersection of seemingly distant and unrelated disciplines and fields. (Remember Einstein?) Making connections among many disciplines often brings an existing product or service into a completely new setting and offers opportunities to those who can see the connection or who bring in new thinking from the far edges of current wisdom. As we urged earlier for your leadership team, so we advise now for your project teams. Have a diversity of backgrounds, experiences, and cultures. Many "old ideas" are given fresh new applications by those who can see new settings, new applications or new twists. This is also why, no matter whether your organization chooses the Creativity or the Discipline school, there will always be a need for a wide variety of Innovation tools and exercises in the ideation phase of Innovation.

Finally, in this messy, sloppy, irrational process of Innovation, also keep in mind the concepts of "sustainable" versus "revolutionary" forms of Innovation. What result does your organization want? As a reminder, car stereo systems and the hundred versions of the SONY® Walkman™ are examples of the relentless flow of sustaining Innovations surrounding some basic products. Revolutionary Innovations seek to change the rules of the game and make current operating models obsolete, outdated, or at risk for future failures. At-home testing kits that replace traditional laboratory tests, TIVO®, and YouTube® are examples of revolutionary Innovations that threaten to replace current models/products, creating entirely new ones seemingly overnight. Clay Christianson has written articles and books on this subject[2], but revolutionary Innovations are difficult to implement and, according to Doblin, should be only six to eight percent of your output from R&D or Innovation efforts. Generally, revolutionary Innovation has to occur far away from existing models and come from outside an industry, because those inside are too tightly bound to the status quo. This is also why the "wrong person/wrong industry" scenario seems to occur so often: those within an industry can't see beyond their current mode. Again, this is another argument for great diversity in Innovation teams in order to see revolutionary opportunity on the edges of existing industries.

Lesson 3: It Is All About Developing Champions

Ideas are great, but without a real champion who believes passionately in the idea, it likely will never get off the ground. Be sure that you have a strong, guiding presence behind each project; otherwise those projects will just sit like so many airplanes stalled on the runway.

> **Champions (n.)**
>
> *1. Those rare individuals who have so much conviction, perseverance, and raw energy that they overcome almost any and all obstacles to get their ideas fully developed and implemented.*

Tom Peters calls champions "monomaniacs with a mission," and they are absolutely essential to the Innovation process. They prevent one of the great dangers of Innovation: an organization becoming an "idea refuge center" for stray, homeless, or ownerless ideas. The ideation process is extremely important and needs time and resources to bring new insights, new thinking, and a rich flow of ideas for future products and services. However, if these great new ideas are not passionately moved through the prototyping and implementation phases by enthusiastic champions, they will surely wither and die in development.

The Innovation Champion's Wish List

‹ Opportunities to Explore

‹ A Supportive, Trusting Environment

‹ Enthusiasm from Leadership

‹ Encouragement to Dream and Reinvent

~~Layers of Bureaucracies, Overhead, and Approvals~~

~~A "Status Quo" Atmosphere~~

~~Stifling Conformity~~

So what does a champion need? Typically, he or she wants the opportunity to refine, experiment, and constantly redesign ideas in an atmosphere of trust, support, and adequate resources. However, this means that bureaucracies, layers of overhead and approvals, and skeptical managers who have a vested interest in the status quo are enormous barriers to organizations genuinely interested in nurturing and growing champions by the dozen. All the well-intentioned policies and procedures that appear necessary to ensure adherence to rules and regulations, to drive out unwanted variation in key processes, and to reduce fraud and abuse, work heavily against the raising and developing of champions. Therefore, since champions don't work well in stifling conformity or homogenous cultures, they are often on the fringes of organizations; they are regularly labeled as freaks, non-conformists, or mavericks. In the least supportive environments, managers may claim that their most innovative people are actually the most difficult, partially because their ideas can be seen as disruptive. This means that in order to achieve long-term success in the field of Innovation, your organization will need to develop a culture that supports both those needing tight rules and procedures and those needing more freedom to dream, experiment, and reinvent.

How do you achieve this balance? At many of the companies we visited, even the ones that depended on a large and regular flow of new, innovative products every year, the leaders spoke about keeping great new ideas just "below the waterline" or just "off the radar screen" until they have strong champions, high level support, and adequate budgets. Otherwise, these defenseless ideas risk being killed or discredited in an early stage by others in the organization. Champions need to be protected and supported early in the process, especially around the prototyping phases when many of the mistakes are worked out and top-level support lined up. This is also why "skunk works" (named after Lockheed Martin's former concept-generating facilities), "bootleg spaces," and small-scale budget adjustments are necessary for developing and growing champions and funding many small experiments.

Also remember that champions can be somewhat unorthodox individuals. They are generally not motivated by extreme rewards or large tangible gifts; rather, their gratification results from working on leading edge technology and programs, and from the sheer joy of seeing their ideas taken seriously and implemented. It often helps to give individuals and project team members occasional lifestyle gifts and rewards, but most often the satisfaction, motivation, and recognition that result from a supportive culture, enlightened leadership, and value-driven results are all that is necessary. Some organizations seem to grow champions by the dozens while others can't find even one. The culture of Innovation, the tolerance for risk and failure, and the enthusiasm for Innovation at the highest levels are the determining factors for growing champions.

Innovation in Action: The Hope Book

Champions are special people; they possess the talents, tenacity, persistence, and passion to carry forward a new idea all the way to implementation. One such champion at Memorial was a staff nurse at the Memorial Regional Breast Care Center. Her project was a book titled Hope: Stories of Breast Cancer Survivors. The nurse's vision was to create a book that contained inspiring stories of hope, as well as a journaling application, that could be handed out to patients newly diagnosed with breast cancer.

This champion presented her book idea several times and was turned down. Using other Innovation tools to re-frame the opportunity and securing donated writing, media, and publication services, she got the project accepted. The book is now handed out free of charge to all new patients. This is a real example of a champion who persisted and "found a way."

Wake-Up Tip:
Celebrate your champions

Lesson 4: There is Failure and Risk in Innovation

Most early research on Innovation distills into a single, core insight. The success of Innovation is often calculated in direct proportion to how many 'at-bats' an organization could have each year. Basically, the theory is that those organizations or individuals who tried more experiments, new ideas, and new products had more successes. Thus, conventional Innovation wisdom almost required a tremendous number of tries, volumes, failures, and hard-earned lessons before a few successes would be possible. (We discussed this "Funnel Theory" of Innovation earlier.) If true, this philosophy requires a large volume of new ideas resulting in numerous failures with only a couple of possible successes. Thus, increasing risk is inherent in launching an Innovation initiative, and an organization beginning the long journey should prepare their boards, staff, and employees for this increase in mistakes, failure, uncertainty, and risk. Let's take a moment to define these key terms so that you can prepare to address them as an organization.

First, be aware that not all risk is the same. Your organization should prepare to identify, recognize, and manage the various types of risks you may encounter. For example, risk can be thought of as the possibility of gain (benefit) or loss and the calculated probability of each outcome occurring. Although it exposes us to the chance of loss or failure, we must acknowledge that especially in today's competitive environment, risk is completely unavoidable, even if we do nothing at all. Risk is a personal or organizational experience, not only because it is subjective, but also because it is the individual (or organization) who suffers the consequences. Risk is an ever-present part of Innovation, and is newly introduced with every idea, business model, or experiment.

Similarly, uncertainty is the possibility that any number of things could happen in the unknown future. It is almost impossible to predict quantitatively what uncertainty means for every new Innovation or product. Champions of new ideas must be willing to accept uncertainty whenever anything new and interesting is tried for the first time. Risk must be evaluated not by the fear it generates in the champion or by the probability of a project's success, but by the value of the goal or new Innovation.

A byproduct of risk and uncertainty are mistakes and failures. As has often been said, the difference between average people and high-achieving people are their perceptions of and responses to failure. Nothing else seems to have the same kind of impact on people's ability to achieve and to accomplish whatever their minds and hearts desire. Redefining and changing our definitions of and our attitudes toward failure is crucial to continuous improvement.

It is also helpful to recognize that there is a wide range of Innovation with characteristics and qualities. The amount of risk and uncertainty is often in direct proportion to where your current project falls on what can be viewed as a Rainbow or Continuum of Innovation, as displayed in Figure 5.3

Figure 5.3 Rainbow of Innovation

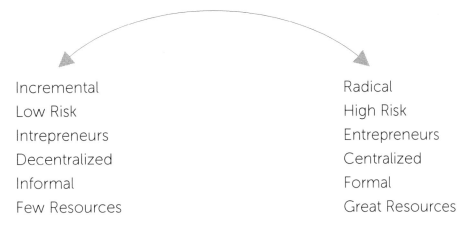

Incremental	Radical
Low Risk	High Risk
Intrepreneurs	Entrepreneurs
Decentralized	Centralized
Informal	Formal
Few Resources	Great Resources

On the left side of the Rainbow are the projects, ideas, and Innovations that are more incremental (or first-order changes). These are the two to eight percent of improvements that add new features and benefits to existing programs and services or marginally improve their impact. The champions of these incremental improvements are often intrapreneurs (those within the organization who produce a steady flow of Innovations to the existing service). Most often, the control for these incremental improvements is decentralized and therefore less risky, less costly to implement, and more reliant on informal application of tools, processes, and experimentation. For example, an incremental Innovation might be to gradually raise customer satisfaction a few points each year. While this is an admirable albeit constrained goal, if teams applied the new tools, processes, and lessons from more radical Innovation, they could more than double or triple their impact for the same effort.

Relatedly, one of the greatest challenges in developing a culture of continuous Innovation is the seeming dichotomy between Quality Improvement (QI) and Innovation Everywhere. QI, by definition, tries to reduce variation of outputs and often has as its goals the standardization of protocols and the elimination of mistakes, errors, and rework. QI seeks to streamline well-defined work processes, eliminate unnecessary steps and sources of errors, and ensure work processes that work the first time, every time according to specifications. Generally mistakes, risks, errors, and unexplained outcomes are eliminated in tight, well-defined work processes. These are the types of improvement that are often achieved by intrapreneurs, and fall on the left side of the rainbow.

The far right side of the Rainbow, however, is different territory. This is where one finds radical Innovation, changes in the rules themselves, and revolutionary technologies that transform entire services and even industries. Radical Innovation is all about making mistakes and trying often startlingly new ideas in a wide range of areas. Fabulous failures are often celebrated in the same spirit that inspired Thomas Edison while struggling to modify the incandescent light bulb. He declared that, "I have not failed. I have successfully found 10,000 ways that will not work."3 Crazy new ideas, weird new combinations from different disciplines, and rapid prototyping (and mistake making) are all hallmarks of the innovative culture necessary to invent, design or create anything interesting in today's competitive environment.

Generally, radical Innovations carry higher levels of risk, can be more expensive to test and prototype, and are often done in partnership with entrepreneurs or larger entrepreneurial organizations. Due to the higher risk and greater expenses, use a more formal, well-defined, centralized structure and business plan process.

Between the two ends of the Innovation Rainbow is a broad continuum covering hundreds of opportunities to innovate, create, redesign and experiment. An organization should be fairly clear as to how much Innovation it really wants to fund, grow, and handle all along this spectrum before it begins. Determining your position is a result of your previous exploration of your culture and of the level to which you accept risk and uncertainty.

Our experience tells us that staff and leadership can always make these distinctions and that peaceful coexistence of quality improvement with radical innovation is entirely feasible. The path to balancing these two priorities lies in moving away from an "either/or" mindset and adopting a "both/and" approach. Jim Collins in his book, Built to Last, devotes an entire chapter to the tyranny of "either/or" thinking and the genius that is released by "both/and" thinking.4 We sell our staff short by assuming that they will not be able to tell when to apply QI tools and principles and when to apply Innovation processes and thinking. Leadership has to be clear on its intentions for each approach; training and education needs to be abundant and constant; and quantifiable measures, outcomes, and feedback loops need to be supplied in order for staff to flourish in this both/and environment. Once established, though, organizations will find a new source of energy, possibilities, and opportunities as they move easily between the disciplines of QI and Innovation.

One way to achieve a balance is to reduce risk on some of the more adventurous Innovations. For example, IDEO, a premier design firm, advocates the use of rapid prototyping and experimentation as a way to significantly reduce the risk in a new venture. This is counter to a traditional approach, which often involves extensive paper analysis, some quantifiable market research, and lots of plans, drawings, and numbers generated before anything is ever built or ready to open. This traditional approach has the greatest risk on the day the new service/ product actually begins or opens and the first real live customer is served. In contrast, the IDEO use of rapid prototyping and experimentation on a small scale with real live, lead customers means that dozens of mistakes are made early and on a small scale. In this way, by the time launch day arrives, the risk of failure is minimal and key customers already know and support the new Innovation. Organizations need space, skills, talents, and experience so that they can develop real competencies in the use of rapid prototyping as a way to lower risks, get customers involved in the actual design of Innovations, and realize astonishing levels of WOW!

Additionally, a Board-approved Innovation Policy helps clarify and make known the level of risk that is acceptable. We will talk about this in more detail in the next chapter. Briefly, however, such a policy provides for the tools and resources necessary to help manage this new risk and its associated increase in failures. Other ways to de-risk project ideas is to involve customers and lead users in the process, use of hands-on simulation software and models, and small scale demonstration models that run for short periods of time. Essentially, every attempt should be made to quantify risk in nearly every new Innovation.

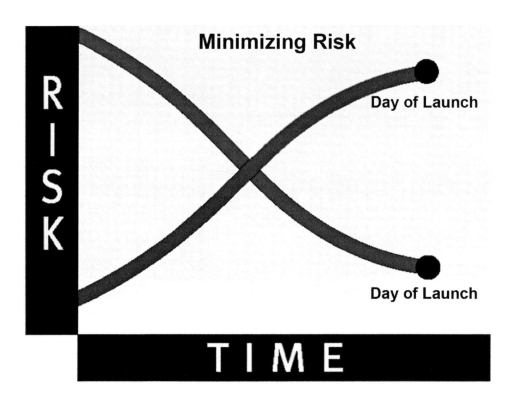

Innovation in Action: HealthWorks! Hummer

One of our favorite examples of rapid prototyping is the development of the HealthWorks! Hummer project. HealthWorks! Kid's Museum was one of our earliest Innovations (see page 117), but was largely oriented toward elementary school children. We wanted to spread health education to middle schools as well, especially since pre-teens' choices and behaviors often resulted in far riskier outcomes. On many levels, HealthWorks! seemed too juvenile, not "cool," and didn't address some of the relevant age and cultural issues (driving, sexual behavior, tattooing and body piercing, etc.).

A small project team began to tackle these important community health issues. First, they began with direct observation, loads of discussions, and small informal focus groups with dozens of middle school students. Early on, the team learned that cars, music, computers, and fashion were of increasing importance and "coolness" to children in this age bracket. The team then began to actively explore how a car could become the vehicle to help deliver the health education messages (curriculum), enabling HW! to meet students on their own turf.

In line with IDEO's method, a small prototype was initially developed (see picture) made from a $20, 6" toy Hummer with glued-on body parts made from play-dough and an old set of eye glasses. This version-1.0 prototype was shown to dozens of middle school kids with the question, "If this Hummer actually drove up on the front steps of your school and the doors were covered with body parts that actually functioned (the heart would squirt red water, the lungs might belch smoke, etc.) and a short health message was delivered to you right there, would you be interested in listening to that?" After enough "cools" the team developed prototype version 2.0, a remote-controlled model that ran around the floor and looked interesting.

About this time, a friend of the team saw the remote-controlled proto-type and said, "I have a friend, Tony Stewart, who might be interested in something like this!" Most of the team didn't know of Tony Stewart, the NASCAR racing legend, but it often happens in Innovation work and with rapid prototyping that unexpected connections result in amazing successes. Two weeks later, two project team members met Tony Stewart; he loved the prototype and the entire idea and asked the magic question, "How can I help?"

With Tony's support and even more positive, constructive feedback from the kids, Memorial launched the HW! Hummer (Version 3.0), which has been taking to the streets, schools, and playgrounds to deliver HealthWorks! messages about making healthy choices. After a few years of wild enthusiasm from kids and their parents, a second HW! Hummer was also launched (a tie-dyed version) to reach even more children. Smaller Hummers (battery powered) completed the family of health educators, and they have spread the health message to more than 4,500 children and audience members.

The key to reducing the risk for this project lay in the first two prototypes. Dozens of changes were made to the Play-dough and plastic versions so that by the time the final version hit the streets, it had the right look, feel, functions, and impact. The fact that it also picked up important financial support and raving fans has come to be a fairly regular unanticipated consequence of our Innovation processes.

Wake-up Tip:
Prototype, Prototype, Prototype!

Lesson 5: Achieve Cultural Transformation!

One of the greatest assets that an organization can develop is a culture of continuous Innovation. As we said earlier, culture is basically "the way we do things around here." It's the unwritten set of rules and practices that define how people act, react, and treat each other in every department and area of organizational life. Cultures can be positive, supportive, energizing, and productive, or they can be negative, defeating, oppressive, and destructive. Since cultures are invisible and hard to measure, they cannot be easily duplicated and they are hard to change. The great innovative organizations have worked hard to develop a positive culture incorporating creativity, idea generation, and experimentation. In order to make the most of an investment in Innovation, an entire organizational transformation will necessitate a tremendous amount of time, energy, and inspired leadership. However, once achieved, the organization will have a renewable asset that will lead to a sustainable advantage for many years.

When an organization begins the long journey toward achieving an Innovation culture, it must be clear to its staff, board, stakeholders, and leaders exactly what its intentions are for undertaking an organization-wide Innovation initiative. Clear intentions are crucial when communicating the need to begin the long journey: what the expectations are for outcomes (both short and long term), and what the impact is expected to be for everyone's job and role in the organization. Organizations with a great deal of trust in their leaders will have a distinct advantage in the early stages until more tangible results can be demonstrated to convince any doubters.

One often hears this well-intentioned question from both senior leadership as well as staff: "Can't we just put our toe in the water first, and just try this Innovation thing on a small scale, to see if it really works?" At best, this is a thoughtful question which tries to see if a small scale effort in just one part of the organization might give some early results that could better demonstrate what Innovation really does, who is best at doing it, and what it looks like when it is successful. At worst, however, the question is a stalling tactic to see if Innovation is just a passing fad, or if there is time to kill it and "get back to the real work."

During our InnoVisits we found little evidence to support the efficacy of sequestering Innovation into one small area of the enterprise. This is partially because most Innovation project teams need to be multidisciplinary and have wide representation from many areas of the organization, e.g., operations, finance, HR, marketing, IT, etc. If only a select few are chosen to experiment with the Innovation methodologies, the initial projects will be less successful due to the limited departmental support on which the team can draw. Plus, Innovation flourishes best in a culture that celebrates and supports Innovation everywhere, with everyday innovators all over the enterprise.

Our team avoided the "toe in the water" approach. Instead, we committed to "sheep-dipping" the entire organization in Innovation. Like its agricultural parallel, which prevents pests in livestock, sheep-dipping an organization involves completely immersing the employees in the ideas, methods, and lessons of Innovation. It makes them part of the mission to create Innovation everywhere.

After all, the only way to truly change a culture is to involve everyone in the adventure, from orientation to training in the methodologies and tools, from the expectations of project teams in every department to the celebration of successes (and fabulous failures) along the way. Culture can change positively with support from the leadership and by fostering a shared need within the organization. You will also need to ensure that the management systems and structures support Innovation, that the Innovation successes receive plenty of attention, and that you sustain them, thereby developing a history of Innovation achievement.

Getting Ready for Implementation

At this point in the journey, you have a clear understanding both of yourself and of the field of Innovation. Now is the time to create your Monday morning implementation plan. In order to see how Innovation can truly change a company, we stop here for a moment (an InnoBreak, if you will) to hear about one of our favorite Innovations: MedPoin*tExpress*. This project has not only had great benefits for us in terms of revenue and partnerships, but more importantly, it has made high-quality care more convenient for our community. Once you have taken this break, we will dig in to some of the nuts and bolts of creating an Innovation culture.

This is the story of
Med Point Express

Three executives are sitting in a conference room and they have just finished WOW Wizard School — our four hour teaching session on the principles and practices of Innovation. They are sitting around talking about new ideas and what they might do as their first WOW project. One of them says to the other, "Hey, I heard about a great new idea. There's actually an urgent care center in a big box retailer, in a Target store, up in the twin cities of Minneapolis/St. Paul and you know what? It doesn't even have a physician!" "WOW, what a cool idea they all said." Now, one of the things they talked about in WOW Wizard School, is when you hear about a good idea you go do something about it. So they grabbed a fourth person, scheduled a flight up to Minneapolis, and began a mystery shopping adventure. One of them had a bad back, sort of, the other one kinda had some sniffles, the third had some vague symptoms of headache and congestion, and the fourth needed an immunization (maybe). Up to the twin cities they went and the first problem is they had a little difficulty finding this new urgent care center. Seems like nobody knew very well where this new facility was. Once they located it, they went into the back of the store and began experiencing the services. What they encountered back by the Pharmacy was a curtain on the ceiling, two chairs, a small table, and a nurse in street clothes. The first urgent care center in American in a big box retailer! One by one they came in hacking and coughing and complaining and whining about one ailment after another. At the end of it, all four of them got back on the airplane came home and had the same conclusion; WOW what a wonderful idea but what a horrible experience! "We can do better," they all said. So back they came to South Bend and began putting in place all the lessons and practices they had learned in WOW Wizard School , The first thing they did was form a WOW project team,

populated with a variety of different people from different disciplines around the organization including parents that actually used urgent care services. They engaged in some brainstorming about what would be a wonderful WOW experience at an urgent care center. After they had developed a pretty good idea, then they began to construct an urgent care center, but they built it entirely out of cardboard in a vacant area in one of our adjacent medical office buildings. When you build it out of cardboard, foam core, sheets, towels, duct tape, every other material they could scrounge up at Memorial, you can make lots of changes without costing anything. And they began to then bring their friends and colleagues in and ask them to go through a simulated urgent care experience and what changes would they to make to the facility and the experience. From there, once they had all the changes down, they constructed model 2.0 which was a real full life model with dry wall, two by fours and so on, but again, in one of our vacant office buildings. After the built model 2.0, they began to ask friends, colleagues, families, co-workers to come in and experience the same type of urgent care visit that they had done previously, and again were able to make changes even to the one that was fully built and developed. Now the big question arose, where should we install one of these and who might be interested in putting urgent care in a major retail setting. Someone suggested "why don't you call the folks at Walmart?" A call was placed and there seemed to be good interest on the part of Walmart and they said come on down to Bentonville and pitch us on putting urgent care centers in Walmarts. Well, whenever you make a presentation, especially to a place like Walmart, it's important that you get your message across quickly and effectively. One of the things that we teach in WOW Wizard School is the three minute elevator pitch. The team worked hard on honing a three minute elevator pitch figuring that they only had about 15-20 minutes with a buyer to get their point across and get some excitement built. Down to Bentonville went the team, and into the very spartant headquarters and they walked right past the little cubicles that held the shabby furniture and most of the buyers and they found themselves in a large conference room when in walked four Vice Presidents and Directors. Nobody gets to see these kinds of folks on a sales presentation. Two and a half hours later after extensive questions and answers and back and forth, Walmart executives said, "build us the very first urgent care center in a Walmart in the United States." Back the team came to South Bend full of excitement and over the next several months the model was created entirely out of cardboard and foam core in the Marketing Department. We used this inexpensive prototype for simulations and to troubleshoot the design. The team also negotiated a lease and on Labor Day, 2005, opened up store number one, the first MedPoint Express in a Walmart in the United States. Store number two in Valparaiso, Indiana, opened a few months later with 5 other sites developed later.

Now for many of you that have never been in an urgent care center in a big box retailer, it works something like this. My twenty year old daughter, Katie, was home from college one weekend and Sunday morning at 8:30 am. She comes tromping down the stairs coughing and hacking and she just felt awful and she looked pretty miserable. I pried open one of her crudded shut eyes, it was bright red, and I made my typical parent amateur diagnosis; Katie had pink eye. Now what do I need as a parent to get rid of pinkeye, I need a couple of prescriptions. It's Sunday morning at 8:30 a.m., what am I to do? Most of us would never call our primary care physicians at that hour, and most of us wouldn't go to an Emergency Room, that inappropriate and very expensive. So what does someone do? Well I did what every good parent in America ought to do, I looked at Katie and said, "gee, you don't feel well, let's go to Walmart!" Doesn't exactly roll off the tongue. "Dad" she said, "I don't want to go shopping, I don't feel well." I said "No, no. Get dressed and I'll show you how we can access some important medical services very close at this hour on Sunday morning." Into MedPoint Express we went. I went over to the side of the store, set me watch, Katie checked herself in, a nurse came out and greeted her, in she went, 16 minutes later she emerged sorta looking a little better but more importantly she had two prescriptions in her hand. She walked right next door to the Pharmacy, they had faxed her prescription ahead, and picked up her prescriptions and she was in and out in 20 minutes for $23. Her dad picked up the bill of course. $15 was all it was for our co-pay because of Memorial's insurance and support for urgent care, and Walmart's $4 per prescription charge. Does that sound like your last urgent care visit or a visit to your last physician? Patients are extremely excited about the MedPoint Express concept in places like Walmart for three reasons. Number one is time: this is the best use of their time, they can get in and out in every visit because of the fixed price board in front of every MedPoint Express and services are designed to get you in and out in 15 minutes. The second reason is convenience. Everyone knows where a Walmart or grocery store is and you don't need any appointment and so it's quite easy for people to know the location and how to access the service. Number three — money; but it's a distant third because even as inexpensive as this is, both time and convenience seems to be bigger factors for people selecting urgent care at MedPoint Express.

We continued to develop our model and streamline our system, responding to team members' ideas and customer needs. Some of the clinics were successful, others were not, but the experience is ours forever to apply to future innovations.

Wake-Up Tip:
Record your lessons for future projects

CHAPTER 6

Structure and Strategy

Strategy is about making clear choices in order to stand out and carefully define your unique value proposition. Although it may often look a little "fuzzy" at the front end of strategy formulation, standing out with well- differentiated offerings is essential in today's crowded, highly competitive marketplace.

Now we S-P-E-E-D up the process, so get ready to create a firm structure and clear strategy for the future of Innovation in your organization. We begin with developing a policy and a team roster, and then we look at how to focus your energy through the use of Importance Screens. In the concluding chapters we will discuss changing your culture, executing your plans, and then measuring your success.

Your Innovation (R&D) Policy

Years ago, we received some wise counsel from a senior CEO near the end of his career. He advised that, "if you really want to change the direction of the organization, have the Board adopt the new direction in a Board-approved policy. Just make sure you don't pursue these Policy adoptions often and make sure they are for really important changes." For us, such a policy was necessary to effect a sustained transformation of our culture.

Board-approved policies carry the highest level of scrutiny and approval, so having one on Innovation is a loud signal to the organization that this new competency is important and crucial for success. Moreover, they are adopted by the governing body and should therefore continue, even if there are changes in senior leadership or market conditions. This means that Innovation will transcend somebody's "good idea" to become a mandated action. Plus, as an added benefit, policies end up on the Board's agenda during meetings and thereby force management to not only report progress regularly, but also to adopt a set of measures/metrics that track progress and form the basis for incentives and compensation bonuses. Such a policy should also have quantifiable results. Specifically, it should help set aside some resources to fund the R&D function, ensuring that the organization has a pipeline full of new programs and services and is regularly investing in new business models. An example of an Innovation Policy is in the appendix.

In addition, a smart way to ensure the Board's hearty support for an R&D function is to involve them in as many of the InnoVisits as possible (see Chapter 4). Nothing takes so much of the risk out of Innovation as going to see firsthand how it works successfully. When Memorial began planning for a major, innovative way to educate kids about health issues (what became HealthWorks! Kids' Museum), we took over 400 community leaders to 23 different sites to look at new models and approaches. With this type of commitment to site visits, the question Strategy is about making clear choices in order to stand out and carefully define your unique value proposition. Although it may often look a little "fuzzy" at the front end of strategy formulation, standing out with well- differentiated offerings is essential in today's crowded, highly competitive marketplace changed from, "should we?" to "when can we get started?"

The need for Innovation as a core competency should also be reinforced with a regular flow of outside speakers and experts, as well as by sending teams to national Innovation conferences or events and by constantly highlighting interesting articles and stories about Innovation from a wide variety of industries and sectors.

Structure for Three Different Pathways

One good approach to structuring Innovation is to trifurcate into three major Pathways. (See Appendix 5) This allows Innovation to remain flexible and easily molded to the different needs of your organization.

THE OPERATIONS PATHWAY

The first Pathway should target everyone in operations and is primarily focused on the 'bubbling up" of great ideas from front-line staff as well as on the major platforms and projects developed by the idea propulsion leaders. Making Innovation a competency (the mission we refer to as "Creating Innovation Everywhere") will be the primary outcome. All departments, companies, and cost centers will break the "commoditization trap" through value-adding differentiation Innovations. All areas can focus on redesigning the critical customer experience in order to increase revenues and market share, as well as dramatically raising customer loyalty through improved customer experiences.

The Innovation budget (up to one percent of net revenues) will support many of these Innovations, but every cost center will be expected to fully participate in implementing a regular flow of Innovations and creative ideas. The Operations Pathway will make extensive use of one of the approved processes such as the WOW! Project Methodology we use for our team member ideas. (see Chapter 7). The Innovation process can be decentralized without a centralized cost center or dedicated Innovation department and should embed Innovation into everyday management practices.

In this context, Innovation is more dependent on its definition as a process than as a goal. Here, Innovation becomes how you create value and excellence for your customers. You will build incentives, rewards, recognition, and training into the traditional line of authority and responsibility system that you have today. All areas of the organization should have access to some financial resources for InnoVisits, prototyping, experiments, and experience redesign.

Projects that grow and become significant (e.g., $50,000+) may need to step up to a separate project track. A set of gurus will be given specialized training with more depth and site visits in order to help consult and advise project champions on the process, use of tools, and training. It is expected that all line directors, managers, and supervisors will be responsible for helping to teach Innovation basics to their staff members and for leading the Innovation initiative wherever possible.

VENTURE CENTER

The second Pathway targets business start-ups and fresh revenue sources for the organization. This is separately organized, and the primary focus is the development of new profits, revenues, or businesses that will help offset the declining profitability of mature products and services. The emphasis of this venture center or Innovation Lab will be to start businesses, partner with existing or new ventures, serve as a "test bed" center for Innovations, or take direct equity or revenue positions for sharing new ventures. The Innovation budget will again serve to fund these projects (up to one percent of net revenues), but unlike the Operations Pathway, there may need to be a small separate staff leading the business development function. The normal spending limits for senior management remain the same.

In the case of strategic alliance, keep in mind that these are more than partnerships; a strategic alliance is a vital relationship formed by two or more entities that hope to walk a path together and achieve an exciting result. They may each walk differently along the path, but they share a common destination based on mutual benefit. The mini-model for such an alliance is:

We need you for _____.
You need us for _____.
Together, we end up with _____.

And, if we find new paths along the way that we can explore together, we will follow them, too.

Some of the advantages to a strategic alliance include:
- upfront cash
- equity/ownership sharing
- revenue sharing

- exchange of services or products
- deep discounting of goods and services

Remember, even if the alliance doesn't reach fruition on one project, being on each other's radar for the future is invaluable. Plus, from every new experience you and your organization will walk away with new knowledge and skills.

The staffing for the new ventures pathway may be unfamiliar territory for many organizations. The types of people you are looking to hire/reorient need to have a variety of complementary skills. First, look for your full-time director. He or she should have a background as an entrepreneur, especially with some new business startup experience. You may also need to partner the director with a contract person or employee with experience as an inventor. He or she will have been through the complex process of experimentation, prototyping, and visualizing techniques. A background in industrial engineering, industrial design, or engineering would be extremely helpful.

Innovation in Action: Chris Endres, Innovator

When Memorial decided to launch a new business venture, Med-Point Express, a line of convenience care clinics, we knew that we were out of our depth. This venture required experience in retail that our current team simply didn't possess. So we looked around but did not find our answer in healthcare. Instead, we found Chris Endres. What skills made Endres so perfect for our needs?

Chris has experience in a number of retail settings including restaurant chains and successfully launching fast food franchises. His fresh retail knowledge was an important enhancement to our team. And, perhaps most importantly, he was enthusiastic to work on this new project. He told us he looked forward to "learning more about how healthcare works." "No!" we practically shouted. "No – we need your fresh eyes and ideas. We know plenty about healthcare, we need your experience in retail." The team we chose to support him answered many of the health-care questions, but Endres was responsible for the successful launch of the clinics and their constant improvement. To learn more about the Med-Point Express journey, see our case study after Chapter 4.

Wake-Up Tip:
Gather great minds.

Industrial design experts and students can also be a great help in the start-up phase. We took advantage of IDEO to design and recruit for the full-time NEW VENTURES DIRECTOR in our organization. You may also need an intuitive observer who has a background in observation skills, human behavior, or anthropology.

This new venture pathways team will serve in a core leadership position to help you launch businesses. They can also serve as gurus or mentors to those in operations who may have an idea that could develop into a business or a significant new revenue source. This team should coordinate new initiatives coming out of the ongoing exploration and networking once they get to a certain stage of development. In most instances the new team will work with the Idea Champion or idea owner to support him or her through the separate Innovation process. Generally, new businesses that have the potential for $10+ million in revenues will be the primary focus. Anticipate that your business start-ups may have an external partner who offers experience, funding, and distribution channels. A small board of three entrepreneurial individuals, the venture center advisory board, may need to meet upon request to review new business start-up projects or approvals for funding. You can also draw on other experienced business or content leaders in your area as a checkpoint to better manage risks and opportunities. At memorial, we developed e2 which is known as the entrepreneurial edge group. We invited entrepreneurs from around our region to be part of this informal group that would come together just a few times a year. We promised to help them meet other entrepreneurs for networking purposes and asked that they allow us to share some of our innovation projects with them confidentially to solicit their fine tuning advice. This has been a mutually beneficial effort and has allowed us access to smart, experienced business thinkers in return for offering them a safe place to talk about ideas.

COMMUNITY PATHWAY

Finally, the third pathway will be for Innovations in the community that improve the quality of life. There are three important reasons to organize your Innovation efforts around a community pathway. First, by discussing what you have learned from others, from InnoVisits, and from readings and seminars, you are continuing to practice and perpetuate an important universal principle: the value of sharing with others. Everyone in the community benefits from your practice of this unselfish principle. The old expression, "A rising tide raises all ships" will come alive for the next generation and for dozens of community businesses and organizations. After all, increasing evidence shows that by sharing your learning and experiences freely and openly, you continue to attract resources, valuable learners, and likeminded leaders who continue to help you and your sharing colleagues along the way. This follows a far-reaching model, the goal of which is to improve not simply the organization, but the world around you.

Figure 6.1: Changing the World with Innovation

↓ Community Pathway helps educate and change community leaders

↓ Community Leaders change their organizations to be more innovative, creative and successful

↓ Organizations help transform communities to be more open to new ideas and possibilities

↓ Communities create the opportunities to help everyone realize his or her fullest potential

↓ Regional Economies develop to better jobs, better economic conditions, and an improved quality of life

Many of our community efforts at Memorial focused on creating health and becoming the healthiest community in the nation; we didn't want to tackle this giant goal alone. Rather, we wanted guidance from engaged, creative partners who shared a similar vision and perspective. Sharing our WOW! Wizard School sessions, inviting community leaders to hear a good speaker who was scheduled to address our organization, and giving speeches to the local service clubs (not for profit and at nearly any business gathering) all helped to reinforce the message of health and wellness for everyone.

Finally, filling an empty seat at one of our training or education sessions costs nothing. Besides, often community attendees contribute unique, helpful insights to the discussion. This diversity helps the idea-generation process, but it also broadens our perspectives outside our field as we plan new solutions and develop new offerings.

For organizations with a commitment to enrich the quality of life in their communities, application of entrepreneurial lessons to community efforts is a great side benefit of an innovative culture. After all, in every community there are health and social problems that never seem to improve. Having teams of people prepared to tackle this problem from a more innovative perspective improves the odds of success. One core way to ignite this effort is to share the tools and serve as a mentor to community agencies working on health and social challenges.

The Basics of Strategy

One of the biggest tasks when leading any complex organization in a rapidly changing environment is to develop a strategic direction that is both compelling and understandable, while also sustaining value for your customers. Innovation strategy is largely about defining how you are going to be distinct from others in your field. It must integrate strong, well-articulated goals and almost become a "cause" for the organization. At the same time, an organization must also continuously improve and strive for excellence in organizational effectiveness.

Doblin's Larry Keeley reminds us to use a disciplined process and carefully select the number of initiatives at which you must excel. They need to be repeatable under a wide set of pressures, conditions, and situations. The use of Innovation protocols (as opposed to only using playful exercises such as brainstorming and blue-sky/blank sheets of paper) will help leaders focus on a winnowed-down number of initiatives.

Therefore, prepare a system that will allow you to create Innovation Platforms. A platform is a broad area of focus that instructs people where the biggest challenges and leverage points are for the organization. Such articulation steers your organization clear of random, unfocused projects that tap into precious energy and time. Instead, you can concentrate on a few carefully selected Innovation initiatives that are bolder, with higher strategic impact and greater long-term importance. When considering your broad Innovation strategy, have small leadership teams focus on the right side of the Innovation Rainbow to determine your platforms, rather than scattering high-level resources among dozens of smaller projects.

Against what criteria should the executive planning team measure the platforms? We found our answer after a visit and conversations with Stephen R. Covey in 2004. We embraced the principles contained in the *Four Disciplines of Execution*: to focus on the wildly important, act on the lead measures, keep a compelling scoreboard, and create a cadence of accountability. As you'll see later, Covey's principles allowed us to effectively organize Innovation goals, measure results, initiate action plans, and establish accountability to achieve real, tangible organizational results. These principles now inform the way we do annual planning, but for the moment let's just address the first aspect: focusing on the wildly important.

At Memorial, Wildly Important Goals (WIGs) have become a common phrase in referring to what is at the top of our "To Do List."

Wildly Important Goal n.

A goal whose failure to be achieved renders any other accomplishments inconsequential. Such a goal requires a significant portion of available resources of time, talent, and money to ensure its success.

Abbr. WIGs

When sifting your competing initiatives, recall your process in crafting a clear and compelling vision, mission, and intent. Aim at taking the organization to a new level of competitiveness and market superiority. This is a huge leap, so keep in mind one of Covey's tools: the importance screen. We use a version of the screen to establish key criteria, thereby enabling senior leadership to reach consensus about which Innovation initiatives are actually important and need top priority in terms of resources, time, and upper-level attention (see Figure 6.3). The framework that results highlights priorities and fosters a robust dialogue leading to team consensus, enthusiasm, and active support. How does it work? As depicted in the figure, the screen clearly and effectively provides the "why" behind the "what" both objectively (the three screens of economic, strategic, and stakeholder) and subjectively (the gut check).

To develop your own platform, you must develop a systematic process of prioritization. This process becomes the way the executive team should make all their decisions on critical goal-setting initiatives. It should include gathering ideas from throughout the organization. The idea generation begins with management soliciting suggestions based on the four Innovation platforms and using a model that incorporates the strategic focus (Figure 6.2) adopted by the executive team.

Traditional brainstorming techniques are useful when identifying potential goals where the organization needs to focus its efforts and resources. If trained facilitators are available in the organization, they should be used so managers can participate in the brainstorming process. The ideas and suggestions generated during the brainstorming sessions throughout the organization should be grouped in one of the four platform categories or strategic focus areas. It is also important to find affinities or similar goal statements and combine them as appropriate.

Once all the ideas and suggestions have been made, they should be gathered for the final selection and prioritizing process conducted by the senior leadership on a dedicated planning day. Prioritizing may take more than one day, and begins by dividing the leadership team into four table groups of four to six people. Since it is not unusual to have 40 or more ideas presented, it will be necessary to "cull" the many suggestions to 12 or fewer candidates. This can be accomplished by having everyone at the planning day vote their top three choices from the list of possibilities. The top 10 or 12 choices become the goals for consideration by each table.

Prior to the planning day it is critical to identify the criteria against which the proposed goals would be evaluated. We identified four major categories of criteria with descriptive statements that were arranged into importance screens for evaluating the goals. Although the descriptive statements under each category may need to be different for different organizations, we encourage use of the Innovation category, especially if Innovation is important to the planning process. The four categories we are recommending as screens are Innovation, Strategic, Stakeholder, and Economic (Figure 6.3).

Figure 6.3: Memorial Innovation Importance Screens: Growth through Innovation

INNOVATION

- Identifies new service or product initiative.
- New philanthropic funds emerge from strategic alliance partners into a Memorial sponsored program.
- The project moves from incremental improvement to radical change in its scope.
- The WOW principles will be applied in its design and execution.

STRATEGIC

- Directly supports organizational Mission, Vision, Goals and Values.
- Leverages core competencies.
- Increases market strength.
- Increases competitive advantage.

STAKEHOLDER

- Increases customer loyalty.
- Ignites the passion and energy of our people.
- Has a favorable impact on partners, suppliers/vendors, and investors.

ECONOMIC

- Grows revenue.
- Reduces cost.
- Improves cash flow.
- Improves profitability.

Any goal or project submitted for significant funding and support by the organization is evaluated against these importance screens. Each of the proposed goals or projects are rated in each category on a scale of -1 to 4 where 4 = high impact, 0 = no impact, and -1 = negative impact. The points for each goal or project are totaled to determine which ones received the most points. Although the numerical ratings provide a good way to measure the importance of each proposed goal, our intuitive ability can also provide valuable insight to the final decision. The last evaluation is the "Gut Check." The final decision is made as a stoplight statement: green = go, yellow = consider, red = reject. An example of a form we used is shown in Figure 6.4.

The goals under consideration are evaluated against predetermined criteria arranged in an importance screen such as in Figure 6.4. Each person should individually complete an importance screen, evaluating each of the 10 or 12 possibilities before discussing them with others at the table. Each table will gain consensus on three WIGs and post them on a flipchart. During the selection process, robust dialogue should be encouraged at the table. Since each person may have significantly different scores (e.g. 16's and 4's), don't waste time talking about candidates that scored low across the board.

After each table has chosen the top contenders, two tables should be joined together and these newly formed larger groups should repeat the exercise, selecting their top three choices. Their decision must be unanimous, which may take some time; however, the extensive dialogue that is sometimes necessary for agreement is a vital step. Everyone must be confident that these goals are the most important. Robust dialogue should be encouraged.

The final step is to have the entire group reach unanimous agreement on the top three goals. It is also important that there be complete understanding of what the goal is intended to achieve. Make sure that the WIGs are "well-crafted" and measurable. The teams should circle in red the words describing the WIGs that are hard to define, too general, vague, or need clarification. The clarification can occur following the planning day, but everyone has to understand and agree on the final wording.

Figure 6.4

MEMORIAL INNOVATION IMPORTANCE SCREENS: Leading Change Through Innovation

SCORING KEY	Innovation SCALE: -1 TO 4	Strategic SCALE: -1 TO 4	Stakeholder SCALE: -1 TO 4	Economic SCALE: -1 TO 4
Worst Best **-1 0 1 2 3 4**				
Use this tool to help identify the two most wildly important goals for you and your team. Rate each category on a scale of -1 to 4. 4 = High Impact, 0 = No Impact, -1 = Negative Impact Use the score totals and your discernment to help you choose the highest priorities.	CONSIDERATIONS:	CONSIDERATIONS:	CONSIDERATIONS:	CONSIDERATIONS:
	• Identifies new product, service, experience or business model.	• Directly supports organizational Mission, Vision, Goals and Values..	• Will deliver value to the customer.	• Grows revenue.
	• Improves an experience, process or procedure.	• Leverages core competencies.	• Passion to pursue is high.	• Reduces costs.
	• The project is something that can be implemented.	• Increases market strength.	• Has a favorable impact on partners, suppliers, vendors, and investors.	• Improves cash flow.
	• Innovation methodologies will be applied.	• Leads to a competitive advantage.	• Improves our level of service and creates "Raving Fans".	• Improves profitability.

Figure 6.4

Candidates for Goals/Projects	-1 0 1 2 3 4 Innovation	-1 0 1 2 3 4 Strategic	-1 0 1 2 3 4 Stakeholder	-1 0 1 2 3 4 Economic	Total Score	Gut Check: Red, Yellow, Green

After consulting with key customers, the executive planning team should meet to make the final selection of goals. In order to wrestle with these decisions, consider an off-site retreat with a trained facilitator. The team will be more focused when conveniently far away from distractions and in a neutral, pleasant atmosphere. The facilitator takes pressure off any one individual and explains the processes for establishing strategy. He or she will guide your team through strategy development via the importance screen. As the facilitator will also emphasize, remember to choose the fewest number of platforms, ones at which your organization can and will truly excel. The entire process takes many hours and may not be accomplished in only one session. There may need to be more of these retreats when leadership is setting new initiatives or during periods of radical change (recessions, new legislation, mergers and acquisition activities, etc.) Most importantly, remember to be focused when setting strategy and selecting platforms; achieve a broad consensus from your senior leadership team. Clarity, urgency, and purpose should be the drumbeats of the process.

The number of exceptional goals an organization can achieve in a given reporting period should be limited to three or fewer. Narrowing the number of goals increases the likelihood that they will be accomplished in a timely and positive manner. Completing multiple projects is not valuable if they are haphazard or slipshod. The competitive market today will not support mediocre products or services.

CHAPTER 7
Processes that Drive Action

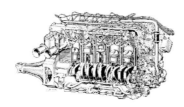

The processes and methodologies used in all Innovation efforts are much like automobile engines. They need to be selected with the end-goals in mind: speed to market, deep insight and lots of muscle, flexibility and economy, or classic style. Remember to select a process that best fits your Innovation intent, and don't fall in love with only the engine (it's just one of many components that drive the organization forward to its destination).

Once the intentions, strategy, and basic structures are in place, identify preferred methodologies and a common language. As you move from thinking about to practicing Innovation, you must identify processes by which the projects can proceed successfully. At Memorial, the processes we embraced evolved over the years and, while your processes will develop organically as well, consider this chapter a jump-start to the engine.

During the initial investigation phase and InnoVisits we saw a variety of tools used at other companies. Some seemed a natural fit for us while others seemed foreign and cumbersome. We poked and prodded our hosts from one organization and another to determine which tools we could introduce to our staff. Then we narrowed down to three methodologies that can launch an effective Innovation strategy. Each of these methodologies or processes was developed by some of the most intelligent and insightful experts in the world. We became quick studies and even quicker networkers with these experts.

Our "scientific" process for selecting tools was to determine compatibility based on a loose rubric:

1. **Clarity:** Could we easily understand and communicate the why and what to our 3600 team members?
2. **Multi-dimensionality:** Did the approach respect all the intellectual and emotional aspects of our business?
3. **Gut check:** Probably the most important but least scientific of all. Did it feel right? Did sparks fly when we connected with these experts and their ideas?
4. **Affordability:** Could we utilize the expertise and tools without breaking the bank?

When you develop your own processes, try these same priorities. Your methods will evolve in a way that best suits your needs. To begin, run the four processes we chose through your rubric and see what results.

We have worked closely with three of the most accomplished and respected Innovation consultants in the world. As a result, we have a unique perspective and skill set that combines the strengths and insights of all three into what we term a "Dream Team Engine." Once The processes and methodologies used in all Innovation efforts are much like automobile engines. They need to be selected with the end-goals in mind: speed to market, deep insight and lots of muscle, flexibility and economy, or classic style. Remember to select a process that best fits your Innovation intent, and don't fall in love with only the engine (it's just one of many components that drive the organization forward to its destination). Exposed to these bright approaches, we never tackled our work the same old way again. Here is an introduction to the methodologies we deployed.

Process 1: Tom Peters, "Passion Trumps Everything."

The first methodology we embraced came from Tom Peters' CALL FOR PASSION. Early on in our journey a number of us attended presentations by this energetic and professionally feisty business consultant. His words were inspiring, his challenges to business leaders made us embarrassed about our blindness and, most of all, his energy regarding our potential was like high-octane fuel for many of us. As we said earlier, he provided us with our wake-up call.

We pursued a deeper understanding of Peters' ideas by calling his group personally. While his lectures and books were enlightening, we knew we needed more information. Creative sparks began to fly during the first call to the Peters group. We were thirsty for ways to get started and they had plenty of proven tools to share. After a number of months of sharing and editing, the foundational methodology we selected had everyone saying (according to Peters' terminology) WOW!

The WOW Project methodology was coined by Tom and his team in his book *The Circle of Innovation*. Companies like us that worked with the Tom Peters Group had access to deeper insights and training so that WOW Project work could become a way of life. We worked closely with their experts to adapt the tools for our industry and then made the decision mentioned in Chapter 5: to sheep-dip the entire organization in this new language and expectation as our best chance at getting things moving in an innovative direction. Thereafter, all members of management were required to take part in a full day of WOW Project training. This training explores ways to move from a typical project management to developing projects that have greater impact, impact we'll remember for the rest of our lives. The create, sell, execute, and move on steps are revealed in brilliant detail, all aimed at fighting mediocrity.

Of course, we needed an innovative way to introduce our Innovation tools, so we developed a package called "Memorial WOW! WIZARD SCHOOL." Imagine lots of methodology wrapped in Harry Potter-like sights and sounds. The five senior leaders who had naturally gravitated toward Innovation from the beginning were established as Head Masters for this new effort. With costumes, handbooks and

Tom Peters' experts on hand, over 200 leaders launched into this historical cultural change.

The core message of our training during WOW Project management was that there is no reason on earth to accept "good enough," to do things the same way we have for years, or to accept things at first glance. If we have the passion, challenging and surpassing the expected norms just comes naturally. Peters asked many of us, "What would it be worth to your organization to have everyone prepared and excited about developing innovative solutions or moving from satisfied customers to raving fans?" Early on, many of us realized we couldn't count high enough to know what this would be worth to Memorial.

Thereafter, we never underestimated the critical role of passion in the innovation process. Many organizations, non-profits and healthcare in particular, are crucially dependent upon the intellect of those who choose this vocation. However, greatness is achieved when the heart of the team member or leader is tied to intelligence. The search for WOW required heart-and-head connections; we had discerned the type of organization we wanted to build.

As we began to see the potential a focus on wow could inspire, the need for intangible qualities (passion, inspiration, personality, and creative design) and tangible qualities (objectives, budgets, and timelines) WERE REQUIRED to achieve a WOW result. In addition, the WOW methodology emphasized other tools that we employed and have discussed (or will discuss):

1. The relevance of tangible as well as intangible aspects of any problem or assignment
2. The importance of integrating diverse views and "freaks" in project work
3. The value of rapid prototyping to make mistakes at lower costs
4. The value of effective concept framing through three-minute pitches
5. The need for understanding the importance of different project stages. The overall wow project process involves the create, sell, execute, celebrate, and move on phases. At first glance they may seem like ordinary project management steps but infact, many organizations spend too much unimaginative time

in execute and miss out the innovation enhancing steps of create and sell. Also, many organizations leave out the celebrate all together as an idea passes from development to operations.

CREATE > SELL > EXECUTE > MOVE ON & CELEBRATE

Establishing this process was the launching pad for building our entire Innovation process. The WOW concept efficiently frames what we were all striving to achieve. Hidden within the simplicity of this approach is a finely tuned attack on mediocrity.

Process 2: IDEO Diving for Depth

The potential of Innovation started to make sense to leaders in the organization, and we had our collective antennae primed to look for other applicable tools. Being ready and able to InnoVisit on a moment's notice led to our relationship with the quirky group known as IDEO. Before meeting the Innovation experts at IDEO's Chicago headquarters, we were curious about why their name kept popping up in articles and presentations we researched. Once we got a first-hand look at the place, the people, and the processes we knew our viewpoints had undergone a complete revolution.

IDEO has been offering product solutions and Innovations since 1991. Back in 2003 when we did our first visit, they were building their services work, and we were happy to be one of their first major clients in our field. From our perspective, IDEO's genius lies in their ability to drill down into the real customer expectations, experiences and unspoken needs.

For example, even though we had already broken ground on our $40 million Heart and Vascular Center construction project, the visit to IDEO prompted us to halt the project until we had a refreshed understanding of customer experiences and needs. This was audacious, but since key leaders and board members could see the power of more innovative solutions, the necessary courage was in place to stop the project and head for destination WOW!

The IDEO approach involved a team of new eyes and brains putting heads together with our staff to guide us to identify opportunities for real improvement. The Deep Dive process, where IDEO team members led intricate observational research, was invaluable for this first project. Their observations were then synthesized, categorized, and shared with a wide project team. The team was comprised of members from within our organization at various levels as well as patients and family members. This prepared us for a variety of hands-on ideation sessions. The sessions were designed to identify the "next level" of solutions we could offer our various customers. The ideation process involved concept reactions, role-playing, and other creative approaches to redefine what was being offered. Special attention to safety, clarity, information exchanges, and customer mapping allowed wild new enhancements to unfold.

As an example of IDEO's close observation seeing afresh what we hadn't noticed, consider their analysis of our cardiac catheterization procedure. Beginning at 6:30 a.m. they watched two separate patients arrive for their day of prep and testing. They reported to the Memorial team that, as they followed these two male patients during their one-day stay, they saw many moments of compassion, efficiency, and attention to detail.

Man A was taken to one room while Man B was escorted to another. As their testing progressed throughout the day the men would sometimes be near one another but never spoke. However, the "Ah Ha!" moment came in the afternoon when Man A was being pushed in a wheelchair one way and Man B was being pushed in the opposite direction. With no notice or words, as their wheelchair rides intersected, the two men spontaneously high fived one another without slowing down their caregivers. Guess what? Having the caregivers slow down to see what's really going on is the entire point. Our IDEO consultants unveiled for us the opportunity to enhance a patient experience by considering the possible positive impact patients can have on one another when going through the same medical situation. By reaching out to one another, they established a camaraderie and silent bond that helped them cope with a rough day in a scary place. Their high-five was a quick moment of celebration that they were both hanging in there.

The lesson for the project team was significant. Despite our dedicated efficiency, attention to common patient comfort details, and clinical expertise, we missed some ways to reduce fear, distract patients from what's uncomfortable, and enrich their sense of wellbeing. It boils down to the old adage of not being able to see the forest for the trees. We are all guilty at one time or another of being too close to see all that's going on. The IDEO Deep Dive processes helped us expand our views and ultimately our ability to differentiate the care we provide.

As a result of our work with IDEO, we created a gathering and educational space for patients and their families. There is plenty of light, flooring laid out in patterns that correspond with walking therapy goals, and a kitchenette where we teach patients how to make heart-healthy meals in their own homes. Here, the idea of a supportive community of patients has been the inspiration; the result has been exceptional.

After completing this Deep Dive project with IDEO, we not only had a much improved cardiovascular project, we also had a handful of in-house staff familiar with the approaches and tools IDEO added to our arsenal. These approaches have been used on many smaller projects since that first engagement. IDEO has also worked on subsequent large projects with us. To develop your own version of this process, keep these core ideas in mind:

1. Small details about how customers live within your organization or use your product can make a big difference on ways to improve and grow. After all, what your customers say can be vastly different from what they actually do.
2. Diverse, objective brain-power provides a fast-track approach for differentiation and unexpected solutions.
3. External contributors with the proper training can push back on your habits and existing policies without worrying about hurt feelings.
4. The wisdom of groups can help identify which ideas are the ones to move on first.
5. With the proper structure and tools, everyone can contribute to innovative solutions.

Process 3: Pine and Gilmore, "All your world is a stage"

The third process of Innovation is based on the book, The Experience Economy, by Joe Pine and Jim Gilmore. They explain that all interactions with customers in service organizations should be as well staged as any performance. The right players, props, sights, and sounds should be selected based on a clearly defined end goal. What will differentiate your offering from competitors, what will make your offering most relevant to customers, and what will recommend the service to others? In 2006, when Pine and Gilmore announced they were ready to take small groups of interested souls and certify them as experience staging experts, we moved quickly and our Vice President of Marketing and Innovation Strategy "graduated" as an Experience Design Expert 003 in 2006, the first certified experience expert in healthcare in the country. We had already read the book, but this new opportunity allowed us to bring their with our operations.

Pine and Gilmore are economists, and the foundation of their methodology is a formula called, "The Progression of Economic Value."

As the model above shows, the more similar your service is to a commodity, the less relevant it is to customers and the less customers are willing to pay for it. For example, when you go shopping for all-purpose flour or white sugar, you tend to choose the least expensive brand; you assume the quality is equivalent across the

Progression of Economic Value

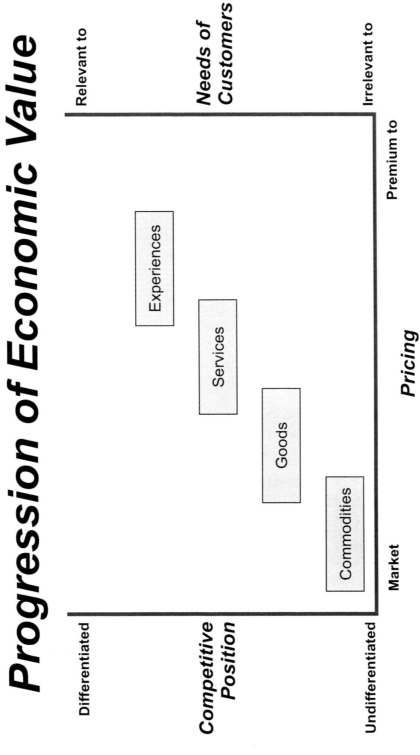

© Strategic Horizons

board. However, when shopping for equivalent honey brands, you may gravitate toward that organic clover-blossom honey, even if it costs a little more or for the cute bear bottle.

As you move up the economic value scale, relevancy increases and pricing can also increase. Most hospitals are stuck in service mode; they believe that offering a great service is the end-of-the-day promise. Honestly, we used to think that too. In fact, over the past 30 years the biggest stretch for many service-based companies has been to dabble in ways of exceeding customer expectations. Based on our study and application of the Pine and Gilmore tools, we now see that we owe our patients, visitors, volunteers, and staff a more well-staged, well-executed experience. We now strive to exceed customer imagination.

Often, these types of Innovation are hard to imagine in the abstract and, when you do imagine them, they can be daunting. One of the most "out there" ideas we ever had was to spend $5 million on a health education museum that would not generate revenue for the rest of the organization. Admittedly, we are a not-for-profit organization, but according to traditional practices, we were more likely to spend our funds on new equipment or on bringing in additional caregivers. Our Innovative idea was to improve the health of the community by trying to keep people healthy, thereby preventing them from needing the hospital in the first place.

Innovation in Action: HealthWorks! Kids' Museum

Back in 1997, our region was rocked by a few high profile child abuse cases in the media. Our physicians were feeling helpless in the face of such a problem and asked the corporation to be more proactive with health education and prevention messaging. They wanted hospital leaders to look for new ways to reach children with information on how to stay well and out of harm's way. Our first big Innovation was a result of this proven need.

However, we knew that we needed to reach children in a different, eye-catching way. The solution germinated after our Vice President of Marketing and Innovation took her 11-year-old son to Discovery Zone, a place where children were engaged in educational playing and exploring. We knew this was the sort of model we needed to follow, that we needed an "edutainment center" that could both engage children and teach them how to stay healthy. Since we were also working on a new fitness complex downtown, we had an opportunity to be more inclusive and balance out the fitness center, focusing on health promotion for a broader demographic – both children and adults.

The team behind what became HealthWorks! Kids' Museum was quickly formed. Our CEO and the idea-generating Vice President quickly initiated a benchmarking effort to see if this idea would fly. What began as a "What if?" discussion blossomed into a 12,000 sq. ft. children's interactive health museum in downtown South Bend. The museum opened in 2000 with 2400 people there to see this wild new idea. To make the experience more memorable, Bill Nye the Science Guy was on hand to celebrate the new model of health and wellness education. In its first decade of operation, more than 400,000 visitors have played in the open exhibit space, sat inside a brain to see how neurons run our lives, and learned about anatomy or drugs in the game-show inspired classrooms.

HealthWorks! Kids' Museum offered more solutions than ever expected. Certainly the come-all policies supported Memorial's not-for-profit mission, as did the emphasis on early prevention. Engaging children to understand how the choices they make early in life impact the quality and length of their lives is central to the mission as well. The tourism-driving facility helped strengthen the developing downtown, and the unique strategy and design served as a marketing tactic to develop a positive relationship between families and Memorial before they ever needed medical services.

Like any good Innovation, the HealthWorks! Kids' Museum involved thinking differently, taking risks (lots of them), bringing together diverse minds for prototyping, and looking beyond what's expected or what's been done in the past. The $5million project also required courage all along the way. This is one of the biggest lessons we learned. The pursuit of an Innovation culture requires the courage to suggest odd solutions, the courage to divert funding away from traditional/safe projects, and the courage to walk a path you've never walked before. This is why courage became one of the initial 3 C's we introduced to you in the orientation. In this case, the payoff will be felt for generations to come. For the children, research shows their visits to the museum have a positive impact on test scores, on decisions whether or not to smoke, what to eat, and whether to wear a helmet when cycling. These results are priceless. Plus, the impact is spreading beyond the South Bend community. In 2009 the first HealthWorks! replication site opened in Tupelo, Mississippi and now thousands of children in that community are benefiting from the off-the-wall suggestion that started in South Bend.

Wake-Up Tip:
Try to change the world.

While this may seem like a crazy concept, focusing on customers' experience, it actually follows an accepted retail/consumer model of expanding customer base as depicted in Figure 7.1.

Figure 7.1.

Awareness – don't know your organization exits

Interest – curious, maybe I'll learn more

Trial – low risk, sample, see what you're like

Active Use – repeat usage, habitual

Raving Fans – passionately tell their neighbors

One key to gaining customer loyalty is to rely on making each customer experience truly exceptional by following Pine and Gilmore's theories. To roll out this valuable process at our organization, all leaders were required to go through an initial orientation to the why, what, and how of experience staging. With our in-house certified experience expert ready to share, some 200 leaders were trained in 2007. Initial exposure then led to a variety of projects where experience design tools helped us to improve and differentiate ourselves from the competition. We also altered some existing policies to reflect our commitment to this new process. Approvals for capital construction or renovation projects now require an experience plan in addition to the facility plan.

To broaden our ability to create exceptional experiences at Memorial, we created a framework that includes a senior staff member certified as an experience expert serving as the "Chief Experience Officer." We also created a training approach to expose staff members at all levels to the experience-staging concepts; staff then become is "Chief Moment Offices."

When you reorient a service organization in order to improve customer experiences, consider creating a theme, using sensory cues as support, developing signature moments, and offering a gift representative of the customer's relationship with your organization.

- **Creating a theme.** A theme is a covert or overt direction that packages the overall experience. For example, our friends at Best Buy's Geek Squad has an overt theme of "secret agent" and a covert theme of "comedy with a straight face." They play up the stereotypical aspects of "geekiness" in order to inspire confidence in their customers, be memorable, and give a cohesive image to their service. Similarly, if you were going to open a restaurant you would have to determine what type of restaurant before too many other decisions could be made. In order to describe the rest of the Pine and Gilmore concepts, let's assume you're in the mood to open an "Old West" restaurant.

- **Supporting Cues.** If we were planning an "Old West"-themed restaurant, the sensory cues to support that theme are fairly straightforward: some cowboy hats, some holsters, and maybe a stuffed bison in the corner. The menu would help explain the theme, offering baked beans, hash browns, and bacon. After all, you can't stage a meaningful experience if customers are confused about what you're trying to offer.

- **Signature Moments.** In order to build raving fans, unexpected pleasant encounters can make all the difference. A signature moment for our restaurant may be a surprise serenade from a staff member for those celebrating an anniversary. Or, couples could be allowed to carve their names into a wooden Wall of Love in the center of the restaurant. A signature moment is a pleasant surprise people remember and didn't expect. It becomes part of a story they can then share with others.

- **Memorabilia.** Offer some tangible item that helps extend the experience beyond the moment. This could be some physical item that serves as a memento or reminder of the experience. Traditionally, restaurants offer matchbooks as you leave; however, be more innovative with your memorabilia. In our hot new restaurant we might offer a photo of the customers with a cowboy, or provide a card with Old West poems to enjoy at home, or maybe we could send leftovers home in a feedbag rather than the traditional brown paper.

Ideas like these can add to the overall customer experience of your organization, but they take careful thought and planning. The results, however, can offer grand competitive advantage.

Innovation in Action: Rejuvenating a Fitness Center

One example of how experience staging was applied to offer an innovative solution is the reframing of a Fitness Center. Observation was added to the experience design tools to build an exceptional new experience around an existing service/facility. This downtown fitness center was about 36,000 square feet and had lost its buzz after being open for ten years. Many aspects of the space could not be changed (location, external presence, space available), but by reworking the internal theme, the center gained as much new energy as the people using it.

Step 1 – Revising the theme: We chose "Balance – balancing what life brings and what your body needs." This theme was flexible enough to evolve with the new technology and offerings the center was developing, while also reflecting the needs of the customer base (working professionals and those recovering from major surgery as well as other, more "traditional" customers).

Step 2 – Sensory Cues: A new yin-yang symbol was applied to the front door. Staff uniforms and printed materials reinforced the ongoing benefits available at the center.

Step 3 – Signature Moments: Birthday messages were sent or given to members with a celebration of balance and what it can mean for their quality of life. Plus, current members were able to see the new look develop, and their shared enthusiasm for the change was a signature moment for the Innovation Team responsible.

Step 4 – Memorabilia: We gave away a balance-themed mouse pad to remind members to stop working and take time for themselves and their health.

Notice that the theme we chose, while overt, was not overwhelming. Themes can be subtle, such as "balance," or blatant, like in our Old West restaurant.

Wake-Up Tip:
Innovation requires a fresh look.

To prepare your version of this process, further investigate Pine and Gilmore's work, both in their book and by studying some companies that have embraced this methodology and benefited from their effort. In addition to the Geek Squad, look at The American Girl Company, Build-a-Bear, and Timberland. And remember, your organization's web presence should be as remarkable as your physical space, so work with your web team on consistency and technical Innovation.

As your sensitivity to experience staging grows, you'll come to realize the difficulty of finding the right theme for the right space, but don't be discouraged: once the overt and/or covert themes are set, the other decisions are much easier. We pursued additional experiential projects as our confidence grew:

New Bariatric Surgery program

Overt Theme: Bridging your Heavy Self to your Healthy Self, respecting the fact that it's not really about the day of surgery but more about the overall journey.

Covert Theme: Each individual is treasured. We learned that many bariatric patients felt unvalued and like outcasts from friends and family because of their weight. Our experience plan sought to help them feel cherished and respected.

New Home Health Anchor Store

Overt Theme: Combining the Art and Science of Medicine for the path you're on. Most people end up at a Home Care store due to some bump in the road.

Covert Theme: In addition to building confidence with the science around the products and services offered, we wanted to add moments of beauty in the site design, and products offered.

Every industry is different, but there are four key paths we consider when creating an enhanced experience designed to delight the customer. For us, because we work in healthcare, we look at ways to demystify, personalize, humanize, and check safety on our interactions and facilities.

It's also important to look beyond the care we've provided to a patient in order to explore how our efforts impact the life of the patients overall. This is where many opportunities to meet new and unexpected customer needs arise. Initially, we looked at trying to exceed customer expectations when developing experience plans; we now try to exceed the customer's very imagination.

CHAPTER 8

Environment

Your organization's environment or culture is key to initiating and sustaining your Innovation adventure. Carefully monitor it through the use of "weather station" gauges and metrics in order to keep your journey on track.

The environment or culture of an organization is crucial to developing and sustaining any new Innovation initiative. It is often made up of visible elements (logos, slogans, awards, buildings, new technologies, products, and services) and hidden, deeply-held sets of beliefs, values, and principles that guide staff and stakeholder interactions .As we explained briefly before, culture is a collection of values, principles, and norms that shape organizational activities and interactions, expressing and informing the character of the organization. Changing this may take many years. For instance, if your organization has always maintained "getting it right the first time, every time," then it may be hard for staff and management to suddenly support uncertainty, risk-taking, failures, and the nonlinear Innovation processes. Senior leadership must make the strong case that creative Innovation should live and thrive, side-by-side with tight, highly disciplined work processes. They must stress that both are necessary for long-term growth and success.

During your InnoVisits, bear in mind the role that environment plays in supporting and nurturing an idea or, conversely, strangling and killing it. While on the

InnoVisit, be sure to probe and analyze the type, strength, and longevity of the organization's culture. Has it changed for good or bad over the last few years? This diagram (8.1), taken from the quality improvement movement, helps to illustrate how easy it is to "borrow" a set of policies, organizational and reporting charts, well-delineated methodologies, job descriptions, and flow charts and yet completely miss how much culture shapes and changes almost all the implementations and strategies.

Figure 8.1

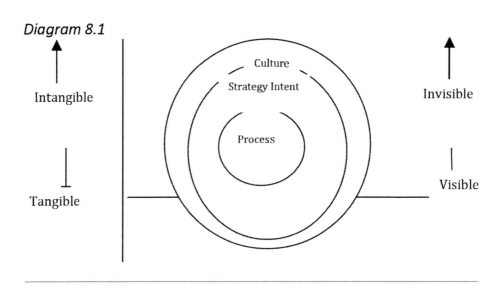

We have run into a few examples where awareness of culture influenced our perception of Innovation practices in host corporations. Often, those corporations that shared some of our environmental characteristics (corporate structure, non-profit status, etc.) Had methods that carried over to ours with few alterations. Sometimes companies with little similarity to ours often had fantastic ideas, but their methods simply didn't align with our culture. Other times having access to leaders in such diverse businesses helped us see our world in a whole new way and we looked for concepts we could apply.

Innovisit: University of Delaware, Lluminari, DuPont

Our network often grows in unexpected ways. One member of our network will connect us to another and so on. For example, our Vice President for Marketing and Innovation Strategy linked us to her connections at the University of Delaware, which had just constructed its own Innovation Park. Mike Bowman, the leader of the park, generously shared the scope and plans of the facility. After learning about us and witnessing our enthusiasm, Bowman connected us with one of his tenants, an ex-DuPont executive who was now heading a start-up women's health company called Lluminari.

We had an excellent conversation with this CEO, and then she referred us over to a safety resource executive at DuPont. After months of discussion about our mutual interests in safety, the resulting strategic alliance between Memorial and DuPont led to their using our hospital as a test site for some of their safety principles. DuPont had over a hundred years' experience proving safety systems in their own industry and some twenty years' experience successfully applying their safety knowledge in industries like automotive manufacturing, aerospace, and aviation. With all the attention to patient safety, healthcare was now on their consulting opportunity list. A few months later, Memorial was in fact selected as DuPont's U.S. test hospital for safety principles.

The one-year alliance gave DuPont real-life understanding of what would work in a hospital setting, and Memorial gained access to new, proven tools and structures that led to improved safety results and landed Memorial on the top five percent safest hospitals in America list within 24 months – another Innovation that will have an impact for years (possibly generations) to come. The alliance included the possibility of Memorial and DuPont partnering to bring consulting services to the healthcare industry; however, changing priorities and leaders at

DuPont stalled the commercialization plan. Currently, discussion about a new healthcare industry safety program continues.

Wake-Up Tip:
Find common ground from which to build

DuPont's culture of safety coincided with Memorial's priorities, and we were able to use the processes of Innovation to create a mutually beneficial partnership. However, changing the culture in your own company can present challenges, which makes the individual and organizational assessments done in Chapter 1 all the more important. They serve as vital monitoring and measuring systems to check on the progress of change, to set crucial milestones, and to detect major setbacks, pockets of resistance, and general backsliding to the old ways. Quick, ongoing assessments help the SET and IPL groups measure how much trust and credibility the staff has in its leaders. Plus, assessments enable them to shift resources to those areas that are struggling the most with the new direction and agenda.

There are six areas of focus when considering how to change an organization's environment and culture; all are important and can play a strong role in shaping the new, more Innovative future.

A. EDUCATION AND TRAINING

Immersing all staff and especially management in initial and ongoing education is probably the most powerful and lasting element of the culture-changing strategy. Memorial began to offer four to eight hours of education, known as WOW! Wizard School, to its entire staff (see chapter 7) to explain the "why" (about the need and key strategies to become more innovative) and the "how to" (the processes, tools, and structures). The training was voluntary for staff but mandatory for those in management. Now, the organization has a shared understanding about the need to make Innovation a core competency, speaks the same language about Innovation, has well understood processes to follow when staff have good ideas, and has a common set of stores, symbols, and TRADITIONS as well as permission to experiment and explore. We also use ongoing speakers and seminars, circulate interesting articles and blogs, continue the InnoVisits, host visiting teams, and attend Innovation conferences and seminars.

B. SPACES AND ENVIRONMENTS

Early on in the Innovation adventure we realized that the spaces in which we normally worked were not ideal for the more interactive, collaborative style of learning necessary for our Innovation initiatives. Most organizations' conference rooms, meeting halls or auditoriums are fairly boring and uninteresting places where innumerable lifeless, boring meetings have taken place over the decades. It is difficult for the same people, going to the same conference rooms to become suddenly creative on demand, using their wildest imagination and their highest energies and passions in these tired old spaces. Therefore, we created the Innovation Café, an interesting, high-stimulus facility that represented a completely new learning environment focused exclusively on Innovation. When a former deli space became available in one of our medical office buildings, it offered the ideal environment in which to begin changing our organization's culture. We incorporated plenty of windows, small moveable round tables, and movable chairs to quickly reconfigure into work groups. The invigorating and interesting displays of our Innovation teachings and processes, great digital media set-ups including music, space for rapid prototyping, and easy access to beverages and snacks was available to the 20–40 attendees using this creative facility. It is a safe place to experiment, think in new ways, dream up novel solutions, create new prototypes of what could be, and express one's curiosity in interesting, imaginative ways. The Innovation Café is also an important symbol to the organization that Innovation is a critical competency which needs to be visible and interesting, that spaces, environments, and experiences really matter, and that business as usual is no longer the norm. The Café became known in the wider community as a great place to visit, to bring teams of colleagues to learn more about Innovation, and to rally for new thinking. Even the Wall Street Journal became interested in this wild, exciting new education facility and featured an article (September 2, 2008) on how a CEO can re-orient an organization around the power of

Innovation. Many new traditions and celebrations have begun all because an exciting space was created that fostered a whole new set of experiences around the Innovation adventure.

"Speed Dating"

One special use of the Innovation Café atmosphere was "Speed Dating." This concept was not to build romances; instead, it was meant to build connections that could lead to innovative solutions. Our first such event had local entrepreneurs and physicians from the Memorial medical staff interacting with science and biotech researchers from the University of Notre Dame and Indiana University School of Medicine – South Bend. Once beverages and hors d'oeuvres were in hand, these experts rotated from table to table in 20-minute increments to learn about one another's work and challenges. Groups explored forming collaborative projects, and the exchange of synergic interests and knowledge led to some short-term solutions with longer-term Innovations sure to follow.

C. VISIBILITY, BRAND AND COMMUNICATIONS

Years ago when our CEO first visited Japan to tour and study the Deming Quality prize-winning companies, he was amazed at how viable and noticeable quality was everywhere in these workplaces and corporate offices. Quality charts, measures, and projects were visible; huge banners and slogans were placed throughout; bulletin boards were filled with quality project team accomplishments; and quality awards and recognitions were used frequently to underline the importance of this competency in all the workers did. Those same lessons need to be applied to the Innovation revolution as well, but not in a superficial way and not in place of years of hard work and difficult decisions. Innovation and the organization's commitment to its principles, practices, and processes needs to be highly visible, highly credible, and highly focused on customer needs as an important element in shaping a new culture.

Developing an Innovation brand that ties back to your vision, mission, and intent is also key in revolutionizing your culture. Your brand should be visible throughout the work and public areas – especially where seminars, teaching, key meetings, and celebrations regularly take place. Some easy ways to build awareness and equity around the commitment to Innovation include:

1. Put the word 'Innovation' in someone's title (see Chapter 6).
2. Develop a short, clear tag line that is used on all Innovation materials. Ours has been, "Innovation Everywhere @ Memorial."
3. Develop graphic standards/symbols that support the tagline – an exclamation point and red ink is used on most of our Innovation material.
4. Title one of your labs or meeting rooms with the word 'Innovation.'
5. Add Innovation goals to all leader expectations.
6. Do annual updates/reports on results from Innovation efforts and include this information in traditional channels of business communication (see Chapter 10).
7. Send news releases to the local media when Innovation projects or milestones are newsworthy.

Regular communications about the Innovation initiatives is essential so that the initiative doesn't seem temporary. The only exceptions should be for those projects that are "off the radar screen," "below the water line," or in "skunk works" status. These designations are usually reserved for those few initiatives that are highly sensitive (either politically or economically), or involve partners who need low visibility and speed in a particular market segment. Team stories, pictures of early/rapid prototypes, even insightful failures need constant visibility through established communication channels to help tell the story of progress on the Innovation adventure. One approach is to hold an Innovation project fashion show where teams display and explain their work and achievements. This can be done on a small or large scale and should combine a sense of accomplishment with a sense of humor.

D. REWARDS, RECOGNITIONS, INCENTIVES

Rewards come in two ways. Intrinsic rewards are those that give great personal satisfaction to the champion and/or the project team members. The excitement of providing a novel solution is often reward enough, especially if it is shared with colleagues and key leadership. Bringing these exciting moments of Innovative accomplishment into the celebration and recognition rituals is a fabulous way to help change culture and generate some new energy around the adventure.

Extrinsic rewards are usually more tangible and physical, and can also be an important symbol in the cultural change process. On one of our early InnoVisits we received some insightful advice: steer away from using money as a motivator and extrinsic reward either for champions or for project team members. The money is soon forgotten– often it is even unrecognized, especially with direct deposit. Monetary rewards also raise internal equity issues with other staff members and tax issues around withholding. A better way to recognize and thank a team is to use lifestyle gifts. These last longer by keeping the reward more visible and useful for longer periods of time. Mountain bikes, interesting furniture, artwork, even building a deck on the back of someone's home can be a significant and long-lasting way to thank a champion. Other creative gifts include cleaning someone's home for a few months, a weekend package to a nearby city, or membership in a health club or spa. The important thing is to build these forms of recognition into your Innovation rituals and ceremonies so that they are regular, highly visible, fun, and provide a forum to talk about the importance and progress of the Innovation adventure.

We have recently begun to highlight four to eight Innovation projects in our annual return on investment reporting (see Chapter 10). At a combined board of trustees and directors meeting, we highlight the accomplishments of the champion and the team, show pictures of their work and outcomes, and then with music and applause the team members go around the room getting and giving "high fives." Team and board members alike remember and talk about this high-energy event; it adds another dimension to the developing culture.

Innovation in Action: Stormy Times, Silver Linings, and Home Runs

October 2, 2008 was a dark and stormy night (figuratively), and Jeff Costello, CFO of Memorial, was on a conference call with Citigroup®. The financial worksheets were in chaos, the stock market was in freefall, and the credit markets were frozen solid (sound like a familiar story?). However, Costello was determined to find some creative way to make the best of these catastrophic conditions. One of the presenters on the call mentioned that floating rate notes (FRNs) which are tax exempt bonds which have floating or variable interest rates, were trading at severe discounts and, since Costello's antennae were up searching for missed opportunities by others, he spotted the silver lining in the otherwise darkening financial storm. He then began to use his well-established network of friends to seek out the innovative range of options, spot the opportunities before others and, most importantly, resist doing what many other colleagues did – hunker down.

Memorial did indeed have $80 million FRNs, so Jeff took action immediately and put together a WOW! Project team in order to seize this unique opportunity. Timing and speed was critical, as was access to cash. Costello bounced his ideas off executives, outside advisors, and board members. Team members were not just internal to Memorial, but included outside representatives from legal, tax, accounting, and rating agencies – all contacted over the phone, on the Internet, and on conference calls, a virtual WOW! Project Team. The central idea and plan was to identify a large holder of these FRNs, in this case a mutual fund desperate for cash, and buy the bonds back at a deep, deep discount near 60 percent of their value.

A special hastily-convened finance committee met and the idea received support. Board members pressed Jeff to make the lowest deal possible since cash was scarce and growing more valuable every passing day. He placed our offer, and within hours the beleaguered mutual fund accepted the offer at 57 percent of their value – an approximate $22 million gain for Memorial's balance sheet. The entire project was completed within six business days. Citigroup acknowledged the transaction as a "home run" during the worst conditions in the financial markets.

However, there were still more opportunities ahead. Memorial was only able to purchase $52 million of the $80 million bond issue; the rest was held by other financial institutions not as desperate for cash. Costello continued to search for additional opportunities, and nearly six months later the owner of the remaining FRNs was now interested in selling. The WOW! Project Team was reassembled, approvals obtained, lines of credit utilized, and tougher negotiations used to repurchase the bonds at a 51 percent discount. As a result, our financial markets began to improve slightly, even though most others were still cautiously waiting. Memorial came through this storm with a $35.4 million improvement in its BALANCE sheet.

Wake-Up Tip:
Always keep your antennae up

The story of the FRNs illustrates several key Innovation practices. First, even in the worst of times, innovative leaders and champions need to search for imaginative opportunities. Second, when you spot an opportunity, act on it with speed and urgency. Third, using the WOW! Project methodology and assembling a talented,diverse (and virtual) team can be essential for a remarkable outcome. Finally, having an innovative culture and the courage to move quickly and boldly can produce "home runs" in unusual places and in difficult times.

E. DIFFUSION OF INNOVATION

Lands' End®, a creative clothing retailer, estimates that they have approximately six weeks after the introduction of a new style or offering before their competition will offer a market-draining imitation. Such diffusion and spread are in stark contrast to the experience of most healthcare delivery or service organizations. This is why innovative organizations like Lands End need a robust pipeline that is full of new products and enhanced offerings to continue to maintain a leadership position in ultra competitive industries like fashion, electronics and food service. Tom Nolan, co-author of The Improvement Guide: A Practical Approach to Enhancing Organizational Performancei compared this dichotomy to two vases, the first of which represents the industry environment. A few drops of dye are added to this water-filled vase. The dye represents some new Innovation that one organization offers or advances. The dye "diffuses" throughout the vase (the entire industry), becoming commonplace and, therefore, embedded. This contrasts to the second vase, filled with gelatin, which represents service organizations. When the dye/Innovation is added to this vase, it rests on the top rather than diffusing. It cannot permeate the environment, and becomes what Nolan terms a mere "island of excellence," without any wide adoption or diffusion.

These two stories are at the heart of the important concept known as diffusion, and it is critical to an organization's success when adopting Innovation as a core competency. In 1962, Everett Rogers published *Diffusion of Innovations*, a book that has become a bible for leaders interested in spreading change throughout their organizations. In this book, he gave a clear definition of the term and its impact on a given field.

Diffusion n.

The process by which an Innovation is communicated among members of a social system through certain channels over time. It has four main elements:

- *It needs to be better than the status quo and simple to understand, demonstrating success on a small scale.*
- *A communication channel must exist through which the innovative idea is spread to potential adopters.*
- *Time is required for effective diffusion.*
- *The structure of the organization can help or hinder the diffusion of Innovations.*

Synonym: *spread*

Another more recent book that became a bestseller is Malcolm Gladwell's *The Tipping Point*. Gladwell compares diffusion of Innovations to epidemics, fashion trends, adoption of technology, and communication challenges. He emphasizes the key role that individuals called "movers" play in spreading change. He also highlights the concept of "stickiness," i.e., why some messages stick, while others do not.

Book Club

Organizational leaders of the Innovation revolution should read Gladwell's and Rogers' books to better understand the challenges and difficulties in spreading Innovations. After some initial education and training in Innovation principles and practices (everything up to now in this book), a good way to focus on the key learning of diffusion/spread is to do a book club over four to six weeks on Rogers' book with your senior leadership team. These sessions help signal to the organization the importance of Innovation as a learned competency and foster the critical leadership principle of continuous learning.

Any student of Innovation will undoubtedly sooner or later come across Rogers' S-Curve of adoption (Figure W). A word of caution is needed in how to interpret the terms in this rather famous statistical distribution curve. The S-curve is a statistical representation of the rate of adoption of Innovations over time in general populations. The small number of innovators and early adopters at the front end of the curve has been rhapsodized with glowing praise by everyone in Innovation cohorts. Those on the other end, the late majority and laggards, are viewed in extremely pejorative terms. As leaders in organizations, we should be extremely careful about "labeling" our work-force and placing value judgments along a narrow slice of an organization's efforts and offerings.

James March, the great management theorist, posited that organizations basically engage in two different sets of activities: Exploration, the search for new knowledge (where Innovation, creativity, and imagination reign), and exploitation, the maximization of payoff from existing knowledge (where existing processes are systematically honed and refined, driving predictable and reliable results).[ii] Organizations need a balance of both activities, and the labeling of those charged with driving out variation in work processes and ensuring reliability and thus high quality of our offerings should not be negatively labeled as "laggards" or impediments to Innovation.

F. TRANSFORMATION AND MATURITY LEVELS

As you have seen thus far, weaving Innovation into every fiber of your organization involves re-examining and revising many aspects of your culture. As we will explain in greater detail in the next two chapters, monitoring progress is essential to achieving goals and providing encouragement. Therefore, finding a way to chart your progress with regard to embedding Innovation should be a consideration. We kept this in mind during and after our work with GE Healthcare Performance Solutions. From them, we learned that organizational transformation is an evolutionary process driven by leaders' passion, time, and focus. The process begins with a focus on activities that build confidence, proceeds to improved business results, and ends with the change becoming part of the organization's culture or

DNA. The graphic below depicts this process and identifies key transformation milestones.

Change – An Evolutionary Process

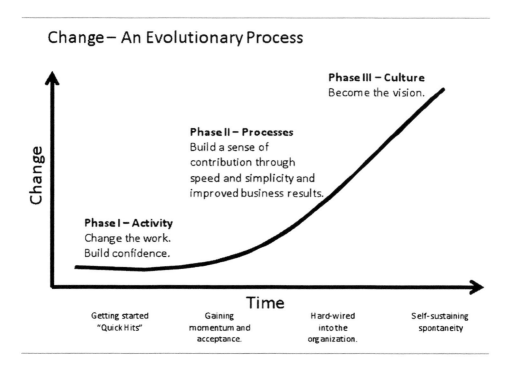

While the conceptual model above is helpful, how do you practically transform your organization and develop innovation as an organization-wide competency capable of producing a sustainable competitive advantage? The best advice we have found appears in an article by John Kotter.[iii] Kotter cites the following eight steps to transforming your organization, many of which are reflected in the steps we have already outlined:

Step 1 – Establish a sense of urgency. Start by examining the market and competitive realities. Then identify and discuss crises, potential crises, or major opportunities. This is similar to the "Wake-up call" presented in Chapter 1.

Step 2 – Form a powerful guiding coalition. Assemble a group with enough power to lead the change effort and encourage the group to work together as a team.

Step 3 – Create a vision. Creating a vision will help direct the change effort. Also, develop strategies for achieving the vision.

Step 4 – Communicate the vision. Use every vehicle possible to communicate the new vision and strategies. Also, teach new behaviors by the example of the guiding coalition.

Step 5 – Empower others to act on the vision. Get rid of obstacles to change. Change systems or structures that seriously undermine the vision. Encourage risk taking and nontraditional ideas, activities, and actions.

Step 6 – Plan for and create short-term wins. Plan for visible performance improvements. Create those improvements. Recognize and reward employees involved in the improvements.

Step 7 – Consolidate improvements and produce still more change. Use increased credibility to change systems, structures, and policies that don't fit the vision. Hire, promote, and develop employees who can implement the vision. Reinvigorate the process with new projects, themes, and change agents.

Step 8 – Institutionalize New Approaches. Articulate the connections between the new behaviors and corporate success. Develop the means to ensure leadership development and succession.

The above can be used as a step-by-step method to change any organization, but what does Innovation look and feel like in an organization that has successfully embedded it and thereby transformed its culture? To answer this, consider is a model of progression or maturity as an organization moves through several stages of embedding innovation within its culture. The model has been built out of Memorial's experience deploying Innovation, as well as knowledge gained from our many InnoVisits.

The model outlines three phases of embedment and describes the evolution of the organization along two dimensions. The first is at an operating-unit level and the second is at a systems and structures level. The time frames at each level are approximate since the speed of progression through each phase depends on a number of factors, such as the leader's passion, time, and ability to focus. The models are designed as a general guideline and not necessarily a prescriptive roadmap for innovation embedment.

THE THREE PHASES ARE:

1. Launch – This is the beginning point where an initial brave few in the organization launch Innovation and craft the embedment strategy.

2. Expanding Impact – Early success has led to other parts of the organization buying into Innovation, and several projects are underway.

3. Cultural Transformation – Innovation is now part of the organization's DNA. Financial and cultural impact is sustained, and Innovation is practiced throughout the organization to solve problems and produce a resilient competitive advantage.

The first model describes what you would expect to see at the operating-unit level within an organization. Simple questions that would typically be asked by employees are presented and answered.

Similar to the above, a maturity model can be presented for the systems and structures necessary to support the innovation embedment.

What you should expect to see at the operating unit level.

	Launch Phase 1 3-18 months	Expanding Impact Phase 2 12-48 months	Cultural Transformation Phase 3 36-60 months
What's the benefit?	Specific problems solved.	New products/services and solutions. Developing leadership skills.	Capability becomes part of the DNA. People attracted & retained by culture. Sustainable competitive advantages.
What are people feeling?	Excitement, discomfort, skepticism.	Experiencing benefits, familiar with tools, building common language.	Professionally and personally enriched, more productive, energized, passionate.
Where's the impact?	Areas & peopled impacted by projects.	Gaining critical mass: significant deployment across organization.	Everyone feels it as part of culture.
What are we measuring?	Progress – number of projects & people trained. Investment Dollars.	Projects results & impact.	Strategic organizational metrics.
Who's leading the effort?	CEO. Top down leadership. Steering committee.	Middle management. Steering committee. 1-2 Champions.	Everyone uses innovation to solve problems and do their work.
What's the focus of the work	Developing the vision and intent. Change management and communication. Implementation planning. Initial training.	Integrate into existing business processes, initiatives and goals.	Hard-wired into organization.

What you should expect to see with systems and structures.

	Launch Phase 1	Expanding Impact Phase 2	Cultural Transformation Phase 3
	3-18 months	12-48 months	36-60 months
Staffing – How will we support the effort?	No full-time resources. Steering committee.	Part-time resources. Steering committee.	1-2 Part-time leaders. Steering committee.
Methodology Selection – How will we select models and partners?	Literature review. Identify models used by other organizations. Consultant review. Develop selection criteria.	Conduct consultant or trainer presentations. Conduct InnoVisits. Select based on criteria.	Continue literature review and identification of models used by other organizations. Attend innovation conferences. Add methodologies as appropriate.
Staff Development – How will we build competency/capability	External trainers. Initial training to all staff (voluntary for staff but not for management).	Content customized to organization. Guru training. Many waves of training across the organization. Mandatory for new employees.	Very large scale. Training completely internalized. Use of in-house gurus as trainers.
Measures – How will we track performance (process & people)?	Process measures (number of projects & people trained, investment dollars).	Outcome measures for overall organization.	Outcome measures for overall organization and business units. Innovation goals & measures hard-wired into performance reviews.

(Con't next page)

Rewards & Recognition – How will we recognize/reward the desired behavior?	Extrinsic – Cash, movie passes, gift certificates.	Extrinsic with lasting meaning – Lifestyle gifts (artwork, furniture, mountain bikes).	Intrinsic – Internal peer based recognition and external public recognition (Board meetings, trade conferences, business clubs, published articles).
Communication Systems – How will information be used to build and sustain momentum?	Book/article club. Leadership days. Road shows to the message out to employees. Open employee forums.	Regular Leadership communication events, internal company publications.	Annual reports, external innovation newsletters and magazines, innovation intranet web portal.
Organization Systems – What information systems are needed?	No change to existing systems.	Supplemental systems developed to interface with existing systems.	Existing systems (HR, Product/Service Development, Financial) are adapted to support innovation.
Information Systems – What information systems are needed?	Simple spreadsheet software.	Project management and tracking software.	Integrated enterprise portfolio and strategy management software. Web-based innovation portals.
Resource Allocation – How will resources be budgeted provided or reallocated?	Board approved R&D Policy. Requests by project champions to steering committee.	Board approved R&D Policy. Budgeted line item at business unit level.	Board approved R&D Policy. Based on strategic innovation platforms.

We hope the above models help organizations considering launching an innovation revolution by serving as a benchmark against which you can measure progress through each phase. Along with the earlier organizational assessments, these should help you gauge areas of strength and opportunities for your embedment strategy. They also show where to aim next, preventing your movement from stalling. Such a plan encourages stakeholders and provides a sense of accomplishment and advancement to your team.

CHAPTER 9

Execution

Execution is almost always the weakest link in the Innovation process. Creating Wildly Important Goals (WIGs) and clear scorecards with great lead and lag measures will keep your initiatives on track and moving ever upward.

Often, those less willing to embrace Innovation say they worry about what they perceive as an ambiguous return on investment (or, in this case, return on imagination). As we said before, to meet this demand for concrete results you must have a consistent, solid process; however, the best methodology is worthless without good execution. Unfortunately, execution is often the weakest link in the rollout of any plan, particularly an Innovation effort.

The problem is that many leaders fail to understand what it takes to convert a vision or an innovative idea into reality. They either don't identify the specific actions necessary, or they fail to follow through to completion. Often, they comment that the details "bore them." Larry Bossidy, Ram Charan, and Charles Bruck emphasize that execution is not a trivial, low-level management activity. It is more like a small tactic than a high-impact discipline and system. Therefore, leaders and Innovation teams need to crystallize their thoughts, anticipate roadblocks, and select people in their organization who can produce results.

Crystallizing one's thoughts requires priorities. We learned the importance of this after years of successful Innovation across the board. The problem was that the number of projects was increasing, but their quality was faltering. After all, when under pressure to come up with projects, people left to their own devices will do anything they can to create new ideas on meeting or anticipating customer needs. This frantic method drains away resources and frustrates people who feel lost in a disorganized system.

At Memorial we became entangled in what Larry Keeley diagnosed as "Innovation fatigue." However, rather than allow Innovation to die out, we checked our gauges and focused on a horizon line: our Platforms.

Now, many organizations can fall back on their mission, vision, and value statements to keep on track, but in some cases, you need one overarching statement that can bring all of these ideas together. It should be a simplified, yet accurate representation of your organization's aims. Ours became, "Make every (patient care) experience exceptional" (Figure 1).It expressed the spirit of the mission,

vision, and values in a clear, concise way and became the call to action throughout the organization.

At Memorial it was decided to provide additional guidance and focus by developing topic platforms for people to direct their efforts. The platforms will be discussed later in this chapter.

Creating Focus

A leader with eight or ten priorities really doesn't know what the most important things are, and neither will anyone else in the organization. The Harris Polling Group[2] surveyed organizations to determine barriers to great performance and discovered that 48 percent of organizations had never decided what were the most important things they needed to do to be successful, and only 15 percent of the people in those 48 percent of organizations could identify what the priorities were. To bring a new idea, program, or goal to life, the entire team needs to be aligned. They need to have a clear line of sight that shows their starting point, their goal, and a plan by which to achieve the goal. To return to our airplane metaphor – they should have an approved flight plan.

Bringing focus and clarity to necessary steps of Innovation can be a greater challenge than one might expect. Like many organizations, Memorial had a practice of asking management for annual goals based on Memorial's six organizational or strategic pillars. In return, we would receive seventy or eighty goals that would be organized into a six- or seven-page annual goals document for board review and approval. Once approved, managers would set in motion the actions needed to accomplish their goals, never really aware of the initiatives of others. The results, although sometimes good, were not always achieved at the highest level of execution. They were often not sustainable, could conflict with each other, and sometimes were not accomplished at all. Simply asking people to identify goals without guidelines and direction from senior management may produce interesting and worthwhile activities, but it does not necessarily translate into acceptable results that are integrated and critical to organization's success.

Depend on your Platforms

Creating platforms for Innovation was an important step in providing focus for our organization. A platform is a broad area of focus that instructs people where the biggest challenges and leverage points are for the organization. Without a platform people go off in any and as many directions as interest them. This is particularly a problem for organizations with limited resources supporting numerous efforts. However, since we had decided our primary objective was to make every experience exceptional, that meant that every initiative had to support that objective in some significant way.

To provide guidance on how that goal was to be accomplished, we chose four major platforms based on patient access, safety, physician access, and follow-up. These platforms were flexible and evolved year after year, but the ultimate goal of making exceptional experiences was always at the forefront.

While it is true that an organization has many responsibilities it is required to fulfill, the critical few items must never be compromised in order to complete transitory assignments and tasks. We have observed that as the number of goals is increased, the level of accomplishment for each goal is diminished.

A couple of issues that often arise during the formation PERIOD are, "How do Six Sigma and Lean fit into an organization's Innovation efforts?" and, similarly, "Can an organization be both highly focused on driving out waste and reducing variation from its work processes while at the same time being wonderfully creative, imaginative, and innovative in launching new products and services?" The answer is that both immensely important methodologies, i.e., Lean/Six Sigma and Innovation, can exist and thrive simultaneously; each plays a crucial role in any organization's future. These two disciplines fuel the pursuit of differentiation and betterment, thereby expanding opportunities for success.

An excellent way to think about these two seemingly contradictory concepts is to explore the vigorous conversation about the topic. Roger Martin, in his book *The Design of Business*[iv],advocates mapping the two different methods onto James March's ideas that,

Organizations may engage primarily in *exploration*, the search for new knowledge, or *exploitation*, the maximization of payoff from existing knowledge.[v]

Both activities can create enormous value, and both are critical to the success of any business organization. Since they can be challenging to engage in simultaneously, organizations often choose to focus on one activity, either exploration or exploitation, to the exclusion of the other and to their own detriment. This again shows both sides of the Innovation and discipline challenge – to excel at operational basics and simultaneously foster creativity, risk taking, and (inevitably) hundreds of failures. Michael E. Porter, strategist at the Harvard Business School, argues that,

> Continuity of strategic direction and continuous improvement in how you do things are absolutely consistent with each other. In fact, they are mutually reinforcing. The ability to change constantly and effectively is made easier by high-level continuity…. The more explicit you are about setting strategy, about wrestling with trade-offs, the better you can identify new opportunities that support your value proposition. Otherwise, sorting out what's important among a bewildering array of technologies is difficult.[vi]

The formulations of strategic distinctions and value proposition goals are complex and difficult to articulate. Porter, however, takes a hard line with the task, forcefully stating,

> Strategy is about making choices, trade-offs; it's about deliberately choosing to be different. Operational effectiveness is about things that you really shouldn't have to make choices on; it's about what's good for everybody and about what every business should be doing…A strategy delineates a territory in which a company seeks to be unique…The essence of strategy is that you must set limits on what you are trying to accomplish: If all you're trying to do is essentially the same things as your rivals, then it's unlikely that you'll be successful.

A broader representative sample of leading strategists and their thinking is listed in Appendix 4.

Innovation in Action: A Strategic Mission

To foster field differentiation and value for our customers, our leadership assigned a mission to the leaders of each of our departments, programs, and support services: use the principles of Innovation to develop your strategies. For instance, how will a given team improve its quality and outcomes, thereby improving the overall quality of our services and setting us far beyond the service offered by our competitors? With such improvement exceed national averages and norms through we continuously focus on our quality improvement efforts (Quality Improvement, Six Sigma/Lean and Baldridge criteria). Our distinction will be boldly underlined if national report cards, Internet transparency, and increasing sharing of clinical, service, safety, and financial performance become WIDELY SHARED, more SCRUTINIZED as a result. Earlier, we made the case that Quality along with Service and Innovation has to be a core competency in order to achieve long-term success. Our ongoing mission to improve our quality is a productive melding of all of these tenets.

Wake-Up Tip:
Stand up and be noticed

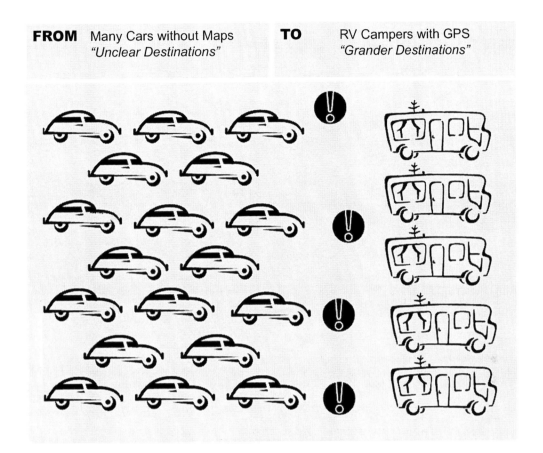

The importance of strategy again underlines the importance of preventing and/or treating the plague of toxic creeping sameness. Leaders need to be continually focusing on the trade-offs, choices, and options for becoming unique, thereby adding value from the viewpoint of their key customers. The principles of Innovation offer the greatest opportunity both to create value and to become distinctive. The balance between getting better and becoming unique can be illustrated by the familiar Figure 6.1.

As Jim Collins reminds us in his book *Built to Last*, the genius is in an organization that can do both simultaneously, as well as creating a competitive, sustainable, peerless advantage in the marketplace. The horizontal axis of our importance screen in Figure 6.1, representing quality Prescription: Stand be and improvement, makes use of the principles and practices of Lean and Six Sigma, Quality Improvement, ISO, etc. This represents the quantifiable results of statistical and data-driven processes. Half of the equation for our service programs and offerings needs to move more to the right on this axis (the quality scale) as quality improves and new techniques, technologies, and practices are adopted.

The vertical axis is where world-class service and Innovation help create value and distinction for your customers. This is where you develop strategies that address your customers' or clients' emotional, mental, and spiritual needs, thereby also creating intangible value that is often the most memorable. As well as moving to the right horizontally, each product or service needs to move continually up the axis to higher levels of distinctiveness with regard to meeting customer needs.

Your future success will be a balance between great products or services that delight your everchanging customers (getting better every day) and a regular flow of new innovative services and products (becoming different). Thus, every product or service has both a quality or improvement plan and an Innovation plan that drives annual outcomes and objectives. As the organization moves increasingly to the right on the better or quality axis as well as up the different or Innovation axis, each of your offerings will generally be moving in a north easterly direction (using a compass for directions). As we said before – we always have our GPS set for Bar Harbor.

Applying the 80/20 Rule

Identifying WIGs does not guarantee results. Without actions and measures to track the progress in achieving the goals, there is little assurance they will be achieved. During Memorial's early years of focus on the wildly important goals, we would often be disappointed by the results, even when we had identified actions to be taken. The thinking had been, "now that we have our goals, we can cross our fingers and focus on tracking the lag measure," confident we would reach our goals.

Focusing on the wildly important goals means you should be placing a significant amount of your weekly time and energy working on actions that are intended to achieve the goals. There will be a tendency for people to add other goals and shift priority away from the WIGs. This should be avoided whenever discovered. We caught ourselves wandering off course when we did a self-review of the calendars of our senior executives. We realized that, while busy, little of our time was actually being spent on directly achieving our WIGs. This became a clear signal that just having an important goal and monitoring it from time to time does not provide any assurance that the goal will be achieved.

This is a problem partially because wildly important goals are lag measures, part of what Covey's book mentions as his second of the *Four Disciplines of Execution.* This means that once the results are known it is too late to correct or change a course of action. What is needed is a timely and frequent indication of the success or failure of measures being taken to achieve the goal or, in other words, advance or lead measures of current activities designed to achieve the goals.

A lead measure is something you can check that is a highly predictive assurance that the lag measure will be achieved. An example is watching your daily calorie consumption in order to lose a desired amount of weight. A lead measure is based on the principle that 80 percent of results come from 20 percent of one's efforts. These 80/20 activities need to have measures that are predictive and can be implemented on a fairly frequent basis, either weekly or daily (Figure 6). A lead measure must answer yes to three questions:

1. Is it predictive with a reasonable level of confidence?
2. Is it able to be implemented frequently?
3. Is the data available?

It only takes a few critical activities to significantly impact the results.

Example of a good and not-so-good Lead Measure.

Not-so-good lead measure:
Measure the number of sales calls made monthly. (If measured monthly, it is too late to course correct by the time the month has closed.)

Good lead measure:
Monitor the number of calls required to make a sale on a weekly basis.

Keep a Compelling Scoreboard

Covey's Third Discipline is to keep a compelling scoreboard. We become serious about our goals when we start keeping score. The scoreboard is compelling when team members are engaged and eager to check progress toward the goal. This means the scoreboard needs to drive team planning and compel action and course correction so the goals are achieved.

Although several electronic scoreboards are available commercially, we chose to design a scoreboard in an Excel format. (Figure 9.2) Our selection was largely a result of considering of what gave us the most information in one place without having to search for supporting documentation. The Excel scoreboard allowed us to drill into the data through links to other information.

Scoreboards have little value if they are not visible to the team and the rest of the organization. So as to be easily accessible, scorecards should be posted in the department, on the company's intranet, and/or distributed through internal mailings.

Creating a Culture of Accountability

Creating and monitoring a scoreboard is directly linked to Covey's fourth discipline of holding each other accountable. This is key to getting the results you expect. Just having identified the most important goals is no assurance that results will follow. Accountability is the key.

We have discovered that being transparent about and proud of our scoreboards adds one such level of accountability. After all, no one wants to be seen as an underachiever, and it should be made clear that these scoreboards are monitored. If no one ever checks on how the organization or team is doing with respect to the goals, people cease to care about commitments. Remember, people are busy with the ongoing demands of the workday: meetings, e-mails, voicemail, etc. Therefore, it is necessary to "hardwire" a regular and consistent process, preferably weekly, to engage in reporting, planning, and follow-through.

Figure 9.2

Memorial WIG Scoreboard – 2010

MAY		Quality	Safety	People	Service	Innovation	Growth	Finance
Hospital		2.00	3.00		2.00			1.00
	YTD	2.00 –	1.00 –		2.00 –			1.00 –
Medical Group		2.00		3.00	3.00	2.00	3.00	1.00
	YTD	2.00 –		3.00 –	3.00 –	2.00 –	3.00 –	1.00 –
Home Care		2.00			3.00	3.00		3.00
	YTD	2.00 –			3.00 –	3.00 ↑		3.00 –
Foundation								1.00
	YTD							1.00 –
Health System								1.00
	YTD							1.00 –

NOTE: Blank entries indicate that data may not yet be completed.

↑ Up   ↓ Down   – Stable

■ 1 - Below Goal   ■ 2 - Approaching Goal   ■ 3 - Meets Goal

Scorekeeping meetings can be informal sessions such as a blackjack stand-up meetings (see Chapter 1) or part of a regular meeting. If the WIG review is to be part of a regular meeting, then the WIG session needs to be placed first on the agenda. This accomplishes several things. First, it reemphasizes the importance of the WIGs and ensures that there will be sufficient time devoted to discussing the progress, successes, or lack of either. At the end of the meeting, people agree about what each person has to do and when.

WIG SESSION CHECKLIST

- ✓ Provide updates on new scores for the lag and lead measures, including the previous week's individual results (both good and bad).
- ✓ Celebrate positive results.
- ✓ Identify corrective actions if needed and set individual goals for the coming week.
- ✓ Identify and get commitment from those who can offer assistance and remove barriers.

Achieving results requires full participation from the entire team throughout the organization. Everyone in the organization should have an understanding of and commitment to the WIGs. The performance of individuals in achieving the lead measures they can influence should become part of their quarterly and annual formal review process. If their performance achieving the WIGs isn't hardwired into their annual review, it will be difficult to get their full commitment to achieving the desired results.

Creating a culture of Innovation requires an established process for executing the organization's wildly important goals. It also requires that the process include an evaluation system for how innovative projects and goals are to be identified and aligned with the organization's mission, vision, and strategies. Finally, accountability is key to creating a culture that achieves results.

CHAPTER 10

Dollars & ROI

One of the primary questions when you begin an Innovation Revolution is "What is the return on investment of Innovation? How do we know this will be worthwhile?" IMAGINE THAT A $2 BILL REPRESENTS $1 OF NEW REVENUE AND $1 OF SAVED EXPENSES. *The $2 Bill Illustration reminds us that it's both new revenues and reduced expenses that help make us the astoundingly high ROI for our Innovation adventure.*

To have a successful Innovation Revolution, you must possess or develop the ability to demonstrate to your finance department, and oftentimes to a skeptical CFO, that Innovation has a positive return on investment (RIO), and that your calculation is credible and based on sound finance principles.

We have often touted the importance of looking to other experienced companies to learn new practices and possibilities. This is especially true when looking for ways to measure ROI. Our journey to measure the "return on imagination" began by benchmarking other innovative companies. We contacted those we had met on prior InnoVisits, or with whom our CEO had relationships, and asked how ROI on Innovation was calculated within their organizations. Some of those companies included 3M®, Guidant®, MedTronic®, IDEO®, DuPont®, Baxter®, Eli Lilly®, Proctor

& Gamble®, Whirlpool®, UL®, WLGore® and Monitor®. We came prepared with a list of questions:

MEASURING ROI: WHAT DO YOU NEED TO KNOW?
- If Innovation is partly driven by unexpected events, to what extent can it be measured?
- What measurements of Innovation are truly meaningful?
- What assumptions underlie any measure of Innovation performance?
- What limitations do you see to Innovation measures?
- Does the benefit outweigh the cost of measurement?
- What are leading companies measuring and why?
- What impact do the measures have on the organization's culture?
- What criteria and measure would you suggest for us?

It was surprising to discover that even leading innovative companies were wrestling with various measures. From the feedback, four major themes became clear:

BENCHMARKED INNOVATION THEMES
- There are as many ways to measure Innovation as there are innovative companies.
- Significant field research is being conducted on Innovation leadership and measurement. Be sure to keep in touch with your Innovation partners to keep on top of new, successful practices.
- Most companies that do have a measuring system focus on levels of investment in R&D.
- There is a high level of interest in learning the "one best way" to measure Innovation, so your ideas will be welcomed in the field.

Let's begin with the methods we've found successful when measuring ROI: staffing models, electronic infrastructure, approvals and resources, ROI calculations. Next, we'll discuss some of the additional Innovation metrics now being used in other companies and which you may be able to adapt to your specific needs.

Staffing Models

There are essentially two basic options for resourcing your Innovation Revolution: the full and part-time models. Each option has strengths and weaknesses that should be considered before choosing which is right for your organization.

FULL-TIME MODEL

The full-time model is analogous to that of most Six Sigma programs; there are full-time positions staffed by individuals of various mastery levels. The Innovation equivalent to a Six Sigma Black Belt is a fully-trained Innovation expert who leads Innovation teams, mentors others doing projects, and works on projects across the organization. The equivalent of a Six Sigma Green Belt is a fully-trained individual who will apply Innovation skills to projects in his or her job areas in the future. They both have key responsibilities and are vital to accurate measurement:

Responsibilities
- Apply Innovation methodologies to projects.
- Introduce methodology and tools to project team members.
- Act as both technical and cultural change agent for Innovation.
- Impact organizational Innovation metrics with successful project management.
- Help deploy Innovation "thinking" into the organization.

There are a number of advantages and disadvantages associated with the full-time model. The central advantage is that you have key people focused full-time on Innovation who truly become Innovation gurus; however, that does mean that these people become expensive resources. They are also the "rate limiter" since the rest of the organization must wait until they become available for projects. Plus, by limiting the potential for Innovation to a select few, you experience similar symptoms to the "toe in the water" approach we discussed earlier: Innovation remains limited and therefore loses its capacity to change the culture.

Part-Time Model

As the name suggests, this model is based on part-time resources. Here, Innovation is part of everyone's job. Don't worry that this leaves Innovation without a focus.

Keep centered with a selected team of leaders drawn from your senior leadership to champion and lead deployment. This leadership team should include vice presidents of marketing, human resources, information systems, customer service, quality, and be lead by the CEO. This team is responsible for leading the Innovation Revolution inside the organization (also see Corner #1 in Chapter 4).

One example of the part-time model in action is that of Doblin Inc., part of Monitor. Their leadership team is responsible for diagnosing Innovation opportunities within the industry, declaring intent or Innovation mission, setting conditions for success, and authoring and fostering Innovation initiatives.

This model is less costly to implement since no additional positions are added within the organization. You are also able to integrate leaders and generate "buy-in" on Innovation as a strategic platform for the organization. Unfortunately, there is no one Innovation "guru" to go to, this method is slower in terms of results generation, and it is highly likely that most individuals within the organization are already overwhelmed with work. Ultimately, it is possible for Innovation to become "one more rock" on an already busy employee's wagon.

So what do we suggest? Answer: Part-time model. It allows you to get started inexpensively. It is also the most effective model for building a culture of Innovation within your organization; everyone is involved and it becomes part of everyone's job.

Once you have chosen the way in which you want to organize, develop a specific staffing structure that aligns with an Innovation category. Exhibit A below identifies our staffing structure based on the category of Innovation.

Exhibit A: Innovation Staffing Structure

Innovation Category	Methodology	Staffing Structure
WOW! Projects	Tom Peters Lean Six Sigma Covey/Education	CEO VP Market Communications & Innovative Strategy Exec. Director, Strategic Alliances
Alliance Development	InnoVisits Venture Capital Tech Transfer	Exec. Director, Strategic Alliances Alliance Lead Legal Risk Management Compliance
Experience Design	Pine & Gilmore IDEO	Certified Design Expert Expeers (facilitators) Chief Moment Officers (CMOs)

The Wow! Projects category is led by the organization's CEO. The CEO is then supported by the vice president of market communications and innovation strategy and the executive director of performance improvement and strategic alliances. As the titles suggest, these are part-time positions overseeing Innovation strategy and implementation.

The Alliance Development Innovation category is supported by a team of experts in addition to the executive director of performance improvement and strategic alliances. This team includes subject matter experts from legal, risk management, and corporate compliance.

The final category, Experience Design, is led by a certified experience design expert, who, in our organization, is also the VP of market communications and innovation and serves as our chief experience officer. This person is supported by two to three individuals who serve as experience design facilitators, called "Expeers," and anyone who has participated in an experience design session (called "chief moment officers" or CMOs).

Electronic Infrastructure

During one of our InnoVisits to 3M, we were strongly advised to we put an electronic infrastructure around as much of our Innovation registration, reporting, and tracking as we could, and to do this as early as possible. This helps leaders take more responsibility and act more quickly and independently. As we said earlier, taking away barriers between your champions and the resources allows the Innovation pipeline to stay open and effective.

An electronic infrastructure also promotes Innovation embedment by providing ready access to information. It shows people that their ideas are valued and, even if not "ready for prime-time," not lost or passed by; it also allows employees the control of managing the process. Plus, it has the added benefit of leveraging the part-time model described above.

How do you get started? To begin, we recommend you avoid building or buying large, unwieldy systems that are difficult to use or maintain. Instead, start with a simple and inexpensive system and then add functionality as your organization matures with Innovation. This means that all it takes to get started is inexpensive spreadsheet software. From this software, three important developmental "dashboards" are helpful to integrate all employees into the Innovation effort while simultaneously tracking the overall status of the organization. These dashboards include a project registry, an Innovation dashboard, and an Innovation pipeline.

PROJECT REGISTRY

The project registry is a simple dashboard that records the following elements:

- Project champion
- Executive sponsor
- Project description
- Expected project benefit
- Anticipated project milestone dates

These elements allow the Innovation leadership team to determine the number of projects over the whole organization, the anticipated benefits, and when the projects should progress through various key milestones.

We started with a simple home-grown version developed by our Web strategist. It was a password-protected system accessed via our intranet. As we matured, we worked with the Tom Peters Company on a strategic alliance with PowerSteering out of Boston to create a version of their software for our Innovation infrastructure. With this system, it is a simple two-step process to register a project. We no longer require a password since it's already secured through our in-house intranet system. The goal is to reduce the number of barriers to registering a project, thereby ensuring that as many of the projects are registered as possible.

INNOVATION DASHBOARD

The output of the registered submissions is a dashboard such as the one shown below. In this case also, it is based on the PowerSteering platform.

This dashboard allows the Innovation leaders within the organization to determine the overall number and types of active Innovation projects. It also identifies the project sponsor and where, by cost center, the project originated. While simple, such a registration system is helpful to determine the type of projects and how they align, or fail to align, with the organization's strategic priorities.

INNOVATION PIPELINE

An Innovation pipeline shows how many ideas are moving towards implementation and how many are shelved or "cryotanked," such as in our earlier example of the Pulse energy drinks in Chapter 4. It tracks the four phases of idea movement from the Wow! Project Management Methodology: create, sell, execute, and move on.

It also allows you to see how many ideas are generated and moving through the pipeline. Exhibit B below shows a summary of our Innovation pipeline. Note that it allows the user to quickly see how many ideas are in which stages of development. It also shows the estimated revenue that could be generated from the projects in the pipeline. The box in the exhibit that says "risk-weighted net income" refers

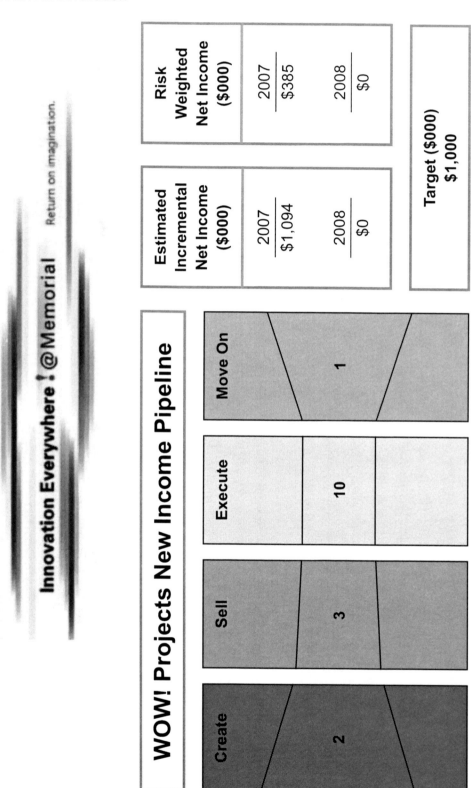

Innovation Everywhere ! @Memorial   Return on imagination.

WOW! Projects New Income Pipeline

Estimated Incremental Net Income ($000)	
2007	$1,094
2008	$0

Risk Weighted Net Income ($000)	
2007	$385
2008	$0

Target ($000)
$1,000

Create	Sell	Execute	Move On
2	3	10	1

AR - Actual Revenue   **CS** - Cost Savings   **LF** - Licensing Fees   **CV** - Contributed Services   **PF** - Philanthropic Funds

Stage/Name	Risk Wgt	Project Lead	Type	Estimated Incremental Net Income ($000)		Risk Weighted Net Income ($000)	
				2007	2008	2007	2008
Create	**0%**						
Nike INSIGHT		M. Krathwohl	AR	—	—	—	—
Nursery Trilogy		C. McCahill	CS	—	—	—	—
Sell	**20%**						
Specworks/SB Choc		D. Stover	AR	—	—	—	—
Seneca Partners-EMS		D. Stover	AR	—	—	—	—
Precious Cargo		P. Smith	CS	—	—	—	—
Execute	**35%**						
ND Intrinsic Motivation		D. Stover	CV	30	—	11	—
Enterprise PACS		B. Ianello	AR	20	—	7	—
Orthopedic/Byme		C. Mueller	CS	820	—	287	—
HWI Replication		B. Zakowski	AR	64	—	22	—
Clinical Trials		K. Emmons	AR	100	—	35	—
ER Time of Svcs Collect		K. Eyster	AR	50	—	18	—
MOM Human Milk Bank		K. Nania	AR	—	—	—	—
Medpoint Express		M. Gordon	AR	—	—	—	—
Memorial Lab		K. Gruber	CS	—	—	—	—
Newbie-to-Do Be		J. Sipp	CS	—	—	—	—
Move On	**50%**						
Innovation Café		P. Newbold	AR	10	—	5	—

to revenue that is adjusted to take into account the probability of success. Net income from early stage projects is projected at a lower dollar estimate than lower-risk projects.

Again, for our first efforts, we decided to go with inexpensive spreadsheet software before progressing to the partnership with PowerSteering. Spreadsheets are not a fancy system, but provide good basic technology to track projects, their movement through development stages, and results.

Innovation in Action: Quickcharts™

As we explained in our InnoBreak, a retail clinic operates within a limited scope of practice. The assessment, diagnosis, and treatment process is driven by strict adherence to evidence☐based protocols, addresses a limited list of problems, and is run by mid-level practitioner without administrative or clerical support. In order to meet our promised time frame, we knew that we would need a technology platform that addressed this unique situation, a "menu option" list of ailments/immunization requests. In addition, the platform would have to be usable by a single person.

The commercially available electronic medical record (EMR) products that might have been used in such a setting were industry leaders designed for use in traditional healthcare care settings. They were too complex and time-consuming.

Therefore, a champion for the project and one of the practice supervisors set to work, drafting, revising, and creating a product that would work. They locked themselves in a room for several days to create the basic template for our fantasy EMR. Then, they moved the templates from poster board to an Excel workbook before driving the Medpoint Express assessment, diagnosis, and treatment protocols into the Excel spreadsheets. They created a unique and amazingly simple workflow. After extensive testing and review, they received executive-level approval for the project and with the help of the Innovation Officer, secured the name Quickcharts.

Raintree Systems® in Temecula, California expressed an interest in meeting with us to discuss the development of this specialized EMR product. Over a 90-day period, the Champion made several trips to their headquarters and worked directly with their product engineers to clarify the workflows and functions.

Within six months, the prototype product was released for testing. The practice supervisor spent the next four months testing every extended function of the Quickcharts EMR product over and over again.

The implementation of Quickcharts into the six retail clinics was a smooth software rollout: no problems and rave reviews from the care providers. The product performs at a level that has exceeded our expectations. A patient record can be entered in five to seven minutes. Within 30 days of releasing the product we had sold two software licenses for Quickcharts.

Wake-Up Tip:
Develop Frameworks
that fit your needs

Approvals and Resources

Be clear about the approval process for projects. We recommend an approach based on the stage-gate process, a conceptual and operational roadmap for moving a new product or service project from idea to launch. It divides the effort into distinct "stages" separated by management decision "gates." Project teams must successfully complete a prescribed set of related tasks in each stage prior to obtaining management approval to proceed to the next stage of development.

We adapted the traditional stage-gate process to the Wow! Project development process, as shown by Exhibit C.

Exhibit C: Project Approval Process

WOW! Project Approval Process

| Champion Generate Idea | Supervisor / Sponsor Pitch | Registering Idea | Applying WOW! Tools & Developing Business Case | Implement Idea |

| Developing Elevator Pitch | Go / No Go Decision | Forming Team | Go / No Go Decision / Supervisor Fuming |

The process begins with the project champion generating the idea and then using one of the Wow! Tools, called the "elevator pitch," to communicate the idea and its benefit to his or her supervisor. We teach team members to boil their idea or solution down to a 2 minute pitch you could give in the time it takes to ride an elevator with a key decision maker. Getting your request down to an easy to understand and passion filled pitch helps clarify the concept for those hearing it for the first time and forces "direct benefit" thinking in the mind of the project champion. At the first gate, the supervisor then makes the decision to proceed with the idea or, if not, ask that it be reframed for greater impact. Once approved by the supervisor, the idea is registered in the project registry and a project team is formed. From there, Wow! tools are applied and a high-level business case is prepared.

WOW! Project Criteria Assessment

Memorial **wow** wizard school

WOW!Projects™

Breifly describe you WOW!Projects™. Review and answer the questions below. In order for your project to be considered as a WOW!Projects™, it must meet at least one criteria listed below. *WOW!Projects™ are revolutionary, beautiful, impactful, create raving fans and are memorable.*

MyWOW!Projects™	Yes/No	How? Or To Whom?	How can this prect be measured?
Adds value to the patient, physician, payor or community.			
Improves the experience and effectiveness of a process			
Improves our level of service and creates "Raving Fans".			
Increases our financial strength, reduces expenses or supports stewardship.			
Helps to develop, attract and retain the Best! Talent.			
Promises a meaningful solution to an important issue.			

Level of personal passion is (Circle 1)	1 Low	2 Lukewarm	3 Medium	4 Warmer	5 On Fire!

Exhibit D: WOW! Project Criteria Assessment

At this point, the project team has reached another gate. If the project requires seed funding to test the idea, the project champion and team presents their case to their supervisor for approval. Currently, vice-presidents within our organization can approve up to $5,000 of seed funding. If the project passes supervisor approval, the project begins implementation.

As mentioned previously and in other chapters, it is important for employees to manage the project themselves. A critical point is to determine if a project is truly a Wow! Project. When developing the elevator pitch, project champions utilize a self-assessment tool to assess the project against our Wow! Project criteria. You should establish a set of criteria for the project methodology you employ. Exhibit D shows.

ROI Calculations

Exhibit X – Wow! Project Criteria Assessment

Now that you have the data and records necessary, you are ready to calculate the ROI from

Innovation. We recommend following the generally accepted definition:

Implicit in this definition is some understanding of "what counts as an Innovation project gain?" We developed criteria in five buckets, as set forth in Exhibit E.

Exhibit E: Innovation Project Gains

What Counts	Explanation
Incremental revenue net of direct costs compared to prior year.	Additional revenue net of direct costs to produce that revenue.
Substantial cost savings.	Cost savings greater than $5K.
Direct fees from licensing agreements.	Fees from strategic alliance agreements.
Contributed services at market value.	Value of services or products received in exchange for using Memorial's resources.
Philanthropic funs from strategic alliances.	Funds donated to Memorial's Foundation as a result of an Innovation alliance.

We also chose to count gains for 24 months after a project is implemented. After this point, we determined that the project would transfer from Innovation to operations.

You should also determine a system by which to calculate the costs of the project. Aim for simplicity. Early in our journey we established a research and development cost center as an outcome of our policy on Innovation. This cost center captures the direct costs of Innovation, such as the costs to run Wow! Wizard School, expenses related to InnoVisits, and certain Wow! project costs such as start-up expenses. At the time of this publication, salaries or other overhead items are not allocated. However, the direct costs of a Wow! project not already captured in the research and development cost center are included.

We also developed a simple process for Innovation teams to "count" the impact of their projects in our ROI calculation. As you'll notice in Exhibit F, this process also relies on the stagegate concept.

WOW! Financial Contribution Process

Complete Online Template		Supervisor Review		Internal Auditor Review		IPL Decision	

START → ⏹ → ⏹ → ⏹ → $

| | Developing Support | | Executive Director Approval | | Developing Pitch | | Record on Scoreboard |

The first step is to complete a simple template on our organization's intranet. The template includes project name, project champion, income type, and a brief description of the project. The completed template generates an e-mail to the executive director of strategic alliances who then begins the review process.

The project champion then generates supporting documents and analyses. These include financial proforma calculations, key assumptions, support for key assumptions, and results to date. The project champion reviews the supporting documentation with his or her supervisor and, if approved, it is then reviewed by the executive director of strategic alliances. We decided that if the ROI is $5,000 or less, no further review is necessary. However, if the ROI is more, we require a review by the director of internal audit. If the impact is $50,000 or greater, all the previous reviews are required as well as a review by the IPL before the project officially "counts" towards the organization's Innovation ROI.

We recommend as few reviews as necessary. Based on the organization's maturity level, fewer reviews mean more submitted projects and greater overall momentum. If there are too many "gates," it may deter project teams from even applying.

Memorial's Return on Imagination

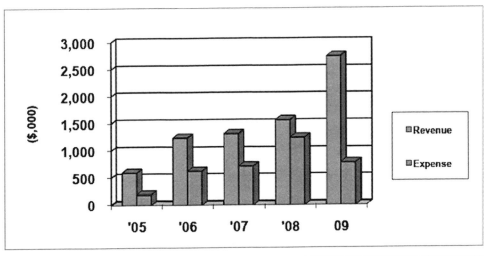

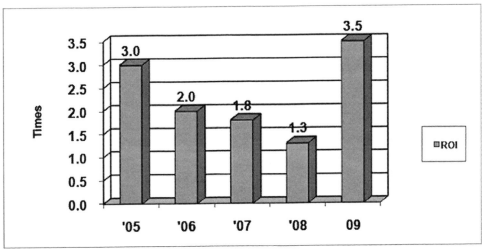

Finance		**Process**	
Business model	Networking	Enabling process	Core process

Offering			**Delivery**		
Product performance	Product system	Service	Channel	Brand	Customer experience

Innovation in Action: Setting High Goals

So, how did we do it at Memorial? First, based on the advice of a senior expert at Proctor & Gamble, we set a large Innovation financial goal, say $1 million each year, and instituted a careful tracking process to calculate the ROI. "You will be amazed at how an organization responds to this challenge. The ROI will shock you!" he had told us during our InnoVisit. Did it happen? Were we amazed? Most definitely. Exhibit X below shows our revenue and expense of Innovation since 2005 while Exhibit Y calculates the ROI. The graphs below show our actual ROI since we began the measurement process in 2005.

While the ROI has decreased since 2005, our revenue and investment in Innovation has increased. This indicates that the organization is investing more in Innovation overall. Each year we at least tripled our income over the cost of Innovation.

Wake-Up Tip:
Set high goals, get amazing results

INNOVATION METRICS

Based on a survey of public company annual reports and our InnoVisits, the following are commonly sued metrics for innovation:

- R&D Spending as a percentage of sales
- Capitalized Expenses as a percentage of sales
- Revenue growth due to new products and services
- Percentage of sales from new products or services
- Number of new products launched in a given period
- Number of ideas or concepts in the pipeline
- Expected future value of ideas in the pipeline
- Number of people trained in innovation methodologies
- The elapsed time from concept of a new product or service to launch.

Conclusion

Our concluding thoughts to those who have stuck with the tale we've shared are that most of all, this was one of the greatest opportunities we could have ever pursued. We are grateful that we were in the right places at the right times to follow one lead after another on the way to understanding the power an innovation culture could grant an organization. That was our initial pursuit, but along the way we also discovered the benefits an innovation mind-set has for one's own job satisfaction, level of engagement, and competency. We've seen this power in action, we've tasted the sweet taste of a great idea, we've heard the heart-felt reactions to a long-awaited solution, and we've felt the energy of a new employee charged up with a sense of what's possible. We can only hope you'll have the opportunity to experience these things too, so get started tomorrow! Our parting guidance is to remember these key Wake-Up Tips we shared throughout the book:

1. Curiosity and courage will take you far.
2. Innovation is always messy.
3. Cultivate diverse views & partnerships.
4. C-suite support is Crucial!
5. Jump in with enthusiasm
6. Record your lessons for future projects
7. Gather experience everywhere.
8. Celebrate your champions.
9. Prototype, prototype, prototype!
10. Gather great minds.
11. Try to Change the world!
12. Be open to fresh looks and new lenses.
13. Find common ground on which to build.
14. Always keep your antennae up for win/win connections.
15. Stand up and be noticed.
16. Develop frameworks that fulfill your needs.
17. Don't be afraid to set high goals for amazing results.
18. Get going. Try something. This week!
19. Be patient for returns.
20. Wake Up and Smell the Innovation!

Appendix 1

TOP INNOVATION BOOKS

1. *The Art of Innovation: Lessons in Creativity from IDEO, America's Leading Design Firm*, Tom Kelley
2. *The Ten Faces of Innovation: IDEO's Strategies for Defeating the Devil's Advocate & Driving Creativity Throughout Your Organization*, Tom Kelley
3. *Re-Imagine: Business Excellence in a Disruptive Age*, Tom Peters
4. *The Circle of Innovation: You Can't Shrink Your Way to Greatness*, Tom Peters
5. *The Experience Economy: Work is Theater & Every Business a Stage*, Joe Pine & Jim Gilmore
6. *Authenticity: What Consumers Really Want*, Joe Pine & Jim Gilmore
7. *The Innovator's Dilemma: The Revolutionary Book that Will Change the Way You Do Business*, Clayton Christensen
8. *The Innovator's Solution: Creating & Sustaining Successful Growth*, Clayton Christensen, Michael Raynor
9. *Seeing What's Next: Using Theories of Innovation to Predict Industry Change*, Clayton Christensen
10. *Leading the Revolution: How to Thrive in Turbulent Times by Making Innovation a Way of Life*, Gary Hamel
11. *Fast Innovation: Achieving Superior Differentiation, Speed to Market and Increased Profitability*, Michael George, James Works, Clayton Christensen
12. *Strategic Innovation: Embedding Innovation as a Core Competency in Your Organization*, Nancy SyndeR&Deborah Duarte
13. *Blue Ocean Strategy: How to Create Uncontested Market Space and Make* Competition Irrelevant, Chan Kim, Renee Mauborgne
14. *Made to Stick: Why Some Ideas Thrive and Others Die*, Chip Heath & Dan Heath
15. *The Wisdom of Crowds*, James Surowiecki
16. *Five Regions of the Future: Preparing Your Business for Tomorrow's Technology Revolution*, Joel Barker & Scott Erickson
17. *Serious Play: How the Best Companies Simulate to Innovate*, Michael

Schrage

18. *The Back of the Napkin: Solving Problems and Selling Ideas with Pictures*, Dan Roam

19. *Presentation Zen: Simple Ideas on Presentation Design and Delivery*, Garr Reynolds

20. *Blink: The Power of Thinking without Thinking*, Malcolm Gladwell

21. *The Design of Business: Why Design Thinking is the Next Competitive Advantage*, Roger Martin

22. *Intrapreneuring*, Gifford Pinchot III

23. *Little Big Things, 163 Ways to Pursue Excellence*, Tom Peters

24. *Unleashing Innovation: How Whirlpool Transformed an Industry*, Nancy Tennant Snyder

25. *The Future of Management*, Gary Hamel

26. *Change by Design, How Design Thinking Transforms Organizations and Inspires Innovation*, Tim Brown

27. *A Whole New Mind: Why Right-Brainers Will Rule the Future*, Daniel H. Pink

28. *Wired to Care*, Dev Patnaik

TOP PERIODICALS ON INNOVATION

1. *Fast Company*
2. *Wired*
3. *Inc.*
4. *Harvard Business Review*
5. *Red Herring*
6. *Fortune*
7. *Forbes*
8. *Scientific American*
9. *HOW/I.D.*

Appendix 2

21 POINTS FOR A SUCCESSFUL INNO-VISIT

1. Why It's Important – Site visits are the most efficient, quickest, and most effective way to increase the learning curve about Innovation. You are learning from those who have been there, often with decades of experience, insight, and learning. It is an excellent way to use scarce time and resources for busy leaders, board members, and physicians. Finally, site visits are energizing and rapidly build support for the new way with key leaders.

2. Three Common Barriers – Big egos from senior management are the most difficult barriers when even considering personally going on an exploration site visit. Having the courage to admit that you don't know much about Innovation and then going personally (as opposed to delegating someone) is the necessary first step in changing your culture to one that supports creativity and new ideas. The second barrier is the fear of looking stupid or naïve in a new field of management. Exploring an unknown territory of the business world can appear scary, but nearly everyone started his or her journey in this same way. Finally, some are intimidated by a perceived lack of knowledge on how to set up the site visit, how to conduct an effective session, and finally how to capture the lessons learned. These 21 points will provide enough to get you started, and after that your enthusiasm for the adventure is all that's needed.

3. Why the Host Company Welcomes You – Your visit will be welcomed by the senior leadership, especially if you are an existing or potential customer for them. Aren't you proud to give tours of your organization and answer questions about how you got to be so successful? Generally, you are visiting those outside your field; therefore, you are not a competitor and, in fact, your charitable mission and vision may be a source of envy for your host. Finally, the host will be flattered that you think they are innovative, that they are being benchmarked against, and that they can help change another industry (that really needs it). Besides, the visit might lead to some new business and strengthen their existing and future relationships.

4. Developing the Prospect List – Start with your existing large suppliers and vendors who are recognized leaders. Identify those with a regular flow of new products and services and an established track record in Innovation. Begin by concentrating on local companies that have R&D budgets. Not only will it be easier to schedule a trip to a local company, but you will also be able sort out new terms and definitions close to home. You will probably need to sit down with your purchasing department and get an idea of your purchasing volumes with major suppliers. This will be necessary information to have in hand before you visit.

5. Stay Away From Sales – Probably the hardest job will be to identify the right person to contact who can then steer you to the R&D or product development leaders. Aim too high and you will not find a sympathetic ear or have problems with tight schedules. Aim too low and you may not be talking to people who actually know the Innovation process and the history of its evolution. Above all, stay away from a pure sales staff, as you will only be viewed as a potential customer and you will receive a very long, elaborate sales presentation.

6. Do Your Homework – Research your site visit company thoroughly. Know how much you are buying from them or one of their competitors. Carefully review their web site, last 2–3 annual reports, top executives, WSJ articles and do a thorough web search. Take along or send in advance a brief description of your organization and its top leadership.

7. Making Initial Contact – Always assign a senior leader to make your initial contact, and be very clear about whom you would like to meet with by title or function (the head of R&D, the person responsible for new product development). Never delegate this responsibility to an assistant, or you might have to use others to make an introduction or initial contact. Always ask at the host company who they think is doing great innovative work and whether they could open some doors or make some contacts for you. Network, network, network!!

8. Explaining Your Purpose – Outline why you are interested in Innovation and why you chose their company. Be clear that you are just learning and would like to bring a small team of senior leaders. Ask for about two hours with their leadership (but almost all of our visits ran much longer, as the passion and enthusiasm take over).

9. Who Goes on the Visit – The small group of leaders who are very passionate and enthusiastic should lead the small team. Always take along an enthusiastic Board member and maybe someone new each time from senior management. An ideal size is 5–6 people, but any size as long as it's not too large can capture the information and build future relationships. Think of these visits as repeatable; always be on the lookout for speakers and presenters for your management education days and Board retreats.

10. Make a List of Questions – Always draw up an extensive list of questions beforehand and share with everyone. At first the questions will be very general, but after a few site visits you will be able to ask better questions and have a compare-and-contrast list from which you can draw. Ask further clarifying questions on any terms or concepts you don't understand. Remember, you are the sponges, and really understanding what the presenter is saying will be key.

11. Sample Questions – Start out by asking who is responsible for new product/service development, what background/training they have, where they go for professional development and meetings, and what literature they read and/or in are published in. Ask what process they use for generating new ideas, where the process originated, who is directly involved in new idea formation, how deep in the organization they go to find new ideas. What are the budget thresholds for new ideas, prototypes or new businesses, and who has to approve what at what level? Finally, ask what are the major obstacles, barriers, and roadblocks that keep them awake at night, that get in the way of the Innovation process? Also ask if they had it to do over again, what would they do differently and what are the lessons learned through the many failures and unsuccessful ventures?

12. Your Objectives – Almost every site visit began with a request by the host for us to clearly set out our hospital's objectives in the journey of Innovation. What did we want Innovation to do for our customers? Be clear as to what your initial objectives are and be prepared to adapt and modify them as your knowledge increases.

13. Non-disclosures – Some organizations may want you to sign a non-disclosure form before they will start the meeting. This protects their intellectual property rights and is a very wise thing to do for all parties. The host takes the protection of this intangible asset very seriously and you should also. You probably will not be able to modify the agreement at all, but you can limit its duration to a year to two.

14. Sponges, Learning, Listening – One of the reasons for having a small group of learners is that often each person has a different perspective on what they heard. Similarly, team members may miss what is being presented because they are sorting out something or taking notes or participating in a side conversation. Try to clarify all aspects of what is presented and always ask what other options or choices were considered each step of the way. Ask if you can get some answers to follow-up questions after you have had a few days to digest what you learned and everyone has had a chance to debrief. This helps with a second visit or important follow-up opportunities and partnerships.

15. Returning the Favor – At first the site visits will be fairly one-way learning, but after a few experiences you may be able to help your host with some new information, new articles, or a web site you discovered. This makes the visit a real win-win for all parties and helps develop your personal network.

16. Opportunities to Partner – Always keep your antennae up for future opportunities to serve as a test bed for new products and services, serve as a beta site for a new prototype, or jointly develop a new product. Being able to spot a good opportunity is a very valuable skill and should be assessed at the end of every site visit.

17. Write Up Lessons Immediately – On the way home or very shortly thereafter, commit yourself to a formal debriefing with as many coworkers as possible. Write down all your observations, lessons learned, steps on the Innovation process, key people you met along with their phone numbers and e-mails, and points for further clarification. Circulate your findings to your senior leadership and enthusiastically review the key points with all those who are interested.

18. Follow-up With Thank-Yous – Always follow-up immediately with a personal thank-you note (never e-mail) to those who shared their experiences. Be sure to let them know how much you learned and how valuable the site visit was to your future planning. Let them know if you have any other follow-up items and be sure to honor your commitments.

19. Small Gifts – Either when you finish the site visit or as a thank-you soon after, it is great to give each presenter a small gift from your organization. The more innovative and clever, the better, so someone should be assigned to come up with just the right gift. Real home run visits should include a great gift basket to express your thanks for sharing so much of their learning.

20. Identifying Contact Persons – Always assign one person to be your organizational chief contact person for follow-up and to really work on the ongoing relationship. Remember to keep your host involved in all your successes (and good failures) and to return any favors from your organization. Watch the business news to follow your hosts' new products and their business successes.

21. Help with Leads and Introductions – Always keep in mind opportunities to supply your host company with important leads for new business. Often, you will know about a new contact that would be valuable to someone in your network. As your partnerships and networks grow, you will become an important organization to many, all because you first started out as a naïve newcomer to the field of Innovation who just picked up the phone and began the exploration.

Appendix 3
BOARD POLICY FOR INNOVATION SUPPORT

Hospitals and Health Systems like other organizations in almost every industry depend on a regular flow of new enhancements to their existing programs and services and a regular flow of new technologies and advancements. Hospitals are beginning to experience many of the same competitive problems that plague other industries;

- a lack of differentiation of programs and services,
- a shrinking operating margin due to many new technologies andentrepreneurial ventures, and
- an increasing shortage of talent in almost every clinical area.

Nearly every industry relies on a vital Research and Development (R&D) function to continuously invent new products and services for the future. R&D is not currently a regular part of America's hospital industry, but Memorial intends to develop this important business strategy for:

- improved health of its community
- to better understand and meet customer needs
- to protect long term financial viability

After studying various industries and many models from some of the most innovative and successful companies around the country, Memorial has identified a set of core principles, defined processes for innovation and idea flow, tools that assist in the creative process, and major elements in the organization's culture that need to be in place. Concomitantly, a dedicated staff focused on R&D and new business start-ups will be necessary as well as financial resources and physical space. Such a new R&D function will necessarily carry a higher risk of financial and customer failure and will require more years of experimentation than many traditional and existing new programs and services.

Therefore, it is the policy of Memorial Health System to establish a new Research and Development function (R&D) to boldly begin the process of innovatively creating new enhancements in community health, a regular flow of innovation in all clinical product lines, and involvement in new related business start-ups. In order to support this vital new investment in Memorial's future, an investment of up to 1% *for capital and operating expenses* of Memorial Health System's net operating revenues will be available to finance these activities. Regular reports on outcomes and progress will become a regular part of management's reporting to the Board.

Approved by Finance Committee - 8/28/02
Approved by Executive Committee of the Board - 8/29/02
Presented proposed revision to Finance Committee – 9/21/05
Approved revision by the Memorial Health System Board – 9/28/05

Appendix 4

PATHWAYS ILLUSTRATION

i   Gerald J. Langley, Ronald Moen, Kevin M. Nolan, Thomas W. Nolan, Clifford L. Norman, Lloyd P. Provost. *The Improvement Guide: A Practical Approach to Enhancing Organizational Performance.* 2nd ed. (Hoboken, N.J.: John Wiley & Sons, 2009).

ii   James March, "EXPLORATION AND EXPLOITATION IN ORGANIZATIONAL LEARNING," Organization science (February 1991)

iii   John Kotter. "Leading Change: Why Transformation Efforts Fail." *Harvard Business Review.* May – April 1995.

iv   Martin, *The Design of Business.*

v   James March. "Exploration and Exploitation in Organizational Learning," *Organization Science* (February 1991), 71-87.

Notes

Notes

Notes

Notes